READINGS FROM
JAVA
DATA STRUCTURES

JOAO AZEVEDO
JAMES CUTAJAR

CENGAGE

Australia • Brazil • Mexico • Singapore • United Kingdom • United States

CENGAGE

Readings from Java Data Structures,
First Edition
Azevedo/Cutajar

SVP, Higher Education Product Management:
Erin Joyner

VP, Product Management: Thais Alencar

Product Team Manager: Kristin McNary

Product Assistant: Tom Benedetto

Director, Learning Design: Rebecca von Gillern

Senior Manager, Learning Design: Leigh Hefferon

Learning Designer: Mary Convertino

Vice President, Marketing – Science,
Technology, & Math: Jason Sakos

Senior Marketing Director: Michele McTighe

Marketing Manager: Cassie Cloutier

Senior Marketing Development Manager:
Samantha Best

Director, Content Creation: Juliet Steiner

Senior Manager, Content Creation: Patty Stephan

Senior Content Manager:
Michelle Ruelos Cannistraci

Director, Digital Production Services:
Krista Kellman

Production Service/Composition: SPi Global

Design Director: Jack Pendleton

Designer: Erin Griffin

Text Designer: Erin Griffin

Cover Designer: Erin Griffin

Cover image: ssguy/ShutterStock.com

For product information and technology assistance, contact us at
**Cengage Customer & Sales Support, 1-800-354-9706
or support.cengage.com.**

For permission to use material from this text or product, submit all requests online at **www.cengage.com/permissions.**

Library of Congress Control Number: 2020904832

ISBN: 978-0-357-63651-0

Cengage
200 Pier 4 Boulevard
Boston, MA 02210
USA

Cengage is a leading provider of customized learning solutions with employees residing in nearly 40 different countries and sales in more than 125 countries around the world. Find your local representative at **www.cengage.com**.

Cengage products are represented in Canada by
Nelson Education, Ltd.

To learn more about Cengage platforms and services, register or access your online learning solution, or purchase materials for your course, visit **www.cengage.com.**

Notice to the Reader

Publisher does not warrant or guarantee any of the products described herein or perform any independent analysis in connection with any of the product information contained herein. Publisher does not assume, and expressly disclaims, any obligation to obtain and include information other than that provided to it by the manufacturer. The reader is expressly warned to consider and adopt all safety precautions that might be indicated by the activities described herein and to avoid all potential hazards. By following the instructions contained herein, the reader willingly assumes all risks in connection with such instructions. The publisher makes no representations or warranties of any kind, including but not limited to, the warranties of fitness for particular purpose or merchantability, nor are any such representations implied with respect to the material set forth herein, and the publisher takes no responsibility with respect to such material. The publisher shall not be liable for any special, consequential, or exemplary damages resulting, in whole or part, from the readers' use of, or reliance upon, this material.

Printed in the United States of America

1 2 3 4 5   27 26 25 24 23

BRIEF CONTENTS

TABLE OF CONTENTS

Welcome to *Readings from Java Data Structures*. This text includes the stand-alone lessons and readings from MindTap for *Java Data Structures* and is intended to be used in conjunction with the full MindTap digital course for a complete learning experience.

MINDTAP COURSE OVERVIEW

MindTap for Java Data Structures is organized into 6 modules. The course is designed to teach students how to write systematic code in Java and improve application efficiency with hands-on practice, step-by-step instruction, and provides immediate feedback and troubleshooting support on their code. Students will develop skills that are in-demand by employers by completing authentic, real-world coding projects that can be added to their GitHub portfolios.

Algorithms and data structures are crucial for application performance. This MindTap teaches problem-solving skills for building efficient applications. It starts with an introduction to algorithms and explains bubble, merge, quicksort, and other popular programming patterns. Coverage also includes data structures, such as binary tree, hash table, and graphs. The course progresses to advanced concepts, such as algorithm design paradigms and graph theory.

Course Objectives:

- Learn about space and time complexities. Express them using big O notation.
- Explore various classic sorting algorithms, such as merge and quick sort.
- Understand the workings of basic (lists, queues, and stacks) and complex (hash tables and binary trees) data structures.
- Gain an insight into various algorithm design paradigms (Greedy, Divide and Conquer, and Dynamic programming).
- Discover string matching techniques
- Master graph representations and learn about different graph algorithms, such as cycle detection, traversal, and shortest path.

MINDTAP COURSE FEATURES

In addition to the readings included within this text, the MindTap course includes the following:

Practice Exercises: Ungraded practice labs presented in an IDE provide an opportunity to practice a new concept in a short coding activity. Students are provided with guided instructional materials alongside a live computing environment.

Lab Activities: Graded coding activities that are completed by a student and contain auto-grading feeds directly to the gradebook. Learners demonstrate an understanding of numerous concepts by completing tasks. Tasks are verified using unit tests, I/O tests, image and webpage comparison, debugging tests, and many other checks.

Module Lab Assessments: At the completion of a module, students are asked to complete a larger, authentic assignment with many tasks that encompasses the learning objectives covered throughout the module. These assessments are partially automatically graded and partially manually graded. Some tasks will be verified using unit tests, I/O tests, image and webpage comparison, debugging tests but other tasks will be unique to each student's project and will require manual grading.

Capstone Lab Assessment: Provides a similar experience to the Module Lab Assessments but occurs at the end of course and incorporates objectives presented throughout the entirety of the course's modules. The goal of this lab assessment is to prove that students have mastered the course's learning objectives. Lab assessments allow students to create programs for their GitHub portfolio.

Module Quizzes: A short multiple-choice quiz at the end of each module encourages students to check their understanding before moving on to the next lesson.

Module Exam: Includes a total of over 350 multiple-choice Test Bank Questions to create tests and evaluate student mastery of each module.

PowerPoint: Students can use the PowerPoints to review key concepts.

Note: Within this text, some coding figures appear to be omitted or skipped. These coding figures only appear in the online lab environment and thus do not appear in the text.

ALGORITHMS AND COMPLEXITIES

MODULE OBJECTIVES

BY THE END OF THIS MODULE, YOU WILL BE ABLE TO:

1. Define an algorithm with an example
2. Measure algorithmic complexity
3. Identify algorithms with different complexities
4. Assess various examples with different runtime complexities

INTRODUCTION

An algorithm is a set of logical instructions to perform a particular task. Algorithms are everywhere nowadays.

As a software developer, understanding the core principles of algorithms and data structures will enable you to make informed decisions on how to approach a particular problem. This is valid whether you're working in a bank writing accounting software or doing medical research data, mining genetic code.

How do we determine which is the right algorithm to use when more than one solution to a problem exists? In this module, we will examine different types of algorithms and discuss how the performance varies in each. We will discuss what makes an algorithm more efficient than another and how to express the complexity of each.

LESSON 1.1 DEVELOPING OUR FIRST ALGORITHM

An algorithm can be seen as a roadmap or a set of instructions to accomplish a well-defined task. In this lesson, we will build a simple example of one such algorithm to help us get started.

Lesson 1.1.1 Algorithm for Converting Binary Numbers to Decimal

Number systems have different bases. Decimals and numbers with a base of ten are what most of us are familiar with. Computers, on the other hand, use only ones and zeros (binary). Let's try to write some code that converts binary numbers to decimals.

Specifically, we want to develop an algorithm that accepts a string containing ones and zeros and returns an integer.

We can convert the binary string by following these steps:

1. Start from the end of the string and process each character at a time. The position of each digit in the binary string corresponds to a decimal number in a sequence.
2. To generate this sequence, you start from one and multiply by two every time, so one, two, four, eight, and so on (see the *Conversion Sequence* row of **Table 1.1**). More formally, the sequence is a geometric progression that starts at one and progresses in a common ratio of two.

Table 1.1   Binary to decimal masking

Conversion Sequence	16	8	4	2	1
Binary String (Mask)	1	0	1	1	0
Result	16	0	4	2	0

3. We then apply the binary string as a mask on this sequence (see the *Binary String (Mask) row* of Table 1.1).
4. The result is a new sequence where the values are only kept if the corresponding position in the binary string has a value of one (see the *Result* row *of* Table 1.1).
5. After applying the mask, we just need to sum up the resulting numbers together.

In the preceding example (Table 1.1), resulting total is 22. This is our decimal number corresponding to the binary number 10110.

 NOTE   To design our algorithm, it's important to realize that we don't need to store the entire conversion sequence. Since we are processing one binary digit at a time (starting from the back), we only need to use the conversion number corresponding to the binary position we are processing.

Snippet 1.1 shows us how we can do this. We use a single conversion variable instead of a sequence and initialize this variable to the value of one. We then use a loop to iterate over the length of the binary string starting from the end. While iterating, if the digit at our current position is one, we add the current conversion variable to the final result. We then simply double the current conversion variable and repeat (see Snippet 1.1).

Snippet 1.1   Binary to decimal. Source class name: `BinaryToDecimal`

```java
public int convertToDecimal(String binary) {
    int conversion = 1;
    int result = 0;
    for (int i = 1; i <= binary.length(); i++) {
        if (binary.charAt(binary.length() - i) == '1')
            result += conversion;
        conversion *= 2;
    }
    return result;
}
```

Test yourself on this concept by completing Lab Activity 1.1: Writing an Algorithm to Convert Numbers from Octal to Decimal.

In this first lesson, we introduced the idea of algorithms by working on a simple example. It's important to note that for every problem, multiple solutions exist. Choosing the right algorithm to solve your problem will depend on several metrics, such as performance and memory requirements.

LESSON 1.2 MEASURING ALGORITHMIC COMPLEXITY WITH BIG O NOTATION

Algorithmic complexity is a way to describe the efficiency of an algorithm as a relation of its input. It can be used to describe various properties of our code, such as runtime speed or memory requirements. It's also a very important tool programmers should understand to write efficient software. In this lesson, we will start by describing a scenario, introducing the topic, and then dive into the details of the various types of complexities and the different techniques to measure them.

Lesson 1.2.1 Complexity Example

Imagine we were given the task of writing a piece of software for air traffic control. Specifically, we were asked to write an algorithm that, in a pre-defined space and altitude, will ring out an alarm if any two aircraft get too close to each other.

In our implementation, we solved the problem by computing all possible distances between every pair in our airspace and keeping only the minimum distance. If this minimum distance is less than a certain threshold, our software will ring out an alarm. The code in Snippet 1.2 shows this solution.

Our little algorithm works fine for a couple of years and the controllers are happy to have this useful alerting. However, over the years, air traffic increases at a fast rate, and instead of having to monitor a few hundred aircraft at any given time, our algorithm has to handle tens of thousands of points. At busy times, the software is having trouble keeping up with the increased load.

We are called in to investigate and we start to write some benchmarks to test how fast the algorithm performs. We obtain the timings shown in **Table 1.2**. As you can see, we are doubling the load on every run; however, our algorithm is not scaling up in the same manner. Our algorithm is not slowing down at the same rate as our input.

Table 1.2   Algorithm benchmark results

Number of Planes	Time Taken (ms)
1000	27
2000	48
4000	190
8000	664
16000	2647
32000	10488

Intuitively, you may expect that if you double the number of planes, then the algorithm will have twice the amount of work to do, and as a result, it should take twice as long. However, this is not what is happening.

When we double the number of planes, the time taken doesn't just double but skyrockets. For example, our algorithm takes 2.6 seconds (2,647 ms) to finish when it's dealing with 16,000 planes. However, if we double the amount of planes to 32,000, the time it takes increases to 10.4 seconds (10,488 ms), a four-fold increase!

In **Figure 1.1**, we plot the benchmark results in a chart. What is going on here? Our algorithm is doing a lot of work due to the nested loop. For every plane point in its input, it's calculating the distance to every other plane. This results in n^2 calculations, where n is the number of planes we are monitoring. We can say that our algorithm has a runtime performance of $O(n^2)$, read as "big O of n squared". Alternatively, we can also call it the quadratic runtime performance (see Figure 1.1).

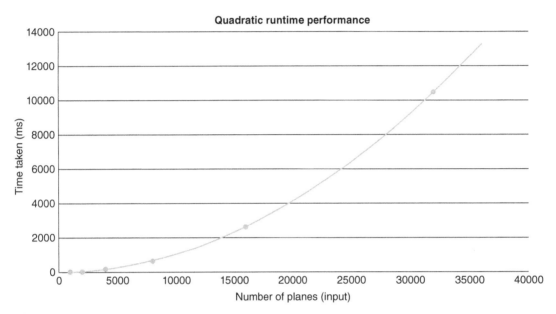

Figure 1.1   Algorithm benchmark result plot

The algorithm listed in **Snippet 1.2** is a slow solution for the closest pair problem. There exists a much more efficient solution that involves a divide and conquer technique.

Snippet 1.2   Minimum distance. Source class name: `ClosestPlane` and `Point`

```
public double minimumDistance(List<Point> allPlanes) {
    double minDistance = Double.MAX_VALUE;
    for (Point p1 : allPlanes) {
        for (Point p2 : allPlanes) {
            double d = p1.distanceTo(p2);
            if (d != 0 && d < minDistance) minDistance = d;
        }
    }
    return minDistance;
}
```

This class of algorithms is explored in *Module 4, Algorithm Design Paradigms*, where we present a faster solution to the closest pair problem.

Increasing the input load on your code does not always mean that the resource consumption will also increase in a directly proportional manner. The relation between the input size of your problem and resource usage (CPU time, memory, and so on) is what this lesson is all about.

In the next lesson, we will see different types of these relations between the problem, input size, and resource usage.

Lesson 1.2.2 Understanding Complexity

To better understand algorithmic complexity, we can make use of an analogy. Imagine that we were to set different types of algorithms so that they compete against one another on a race track. However, there is a slight twist: The race course has no finish line.

Since the race is infinite, the aim of the race is to surpass the other, slower opponents over time race is infinite so it doesn't finish. In this analogy, the race track distance is our algorithm input. How far from the start we get, after a certain amount of time, represents the amount of work done by our code.

Recall the quadratic method for measuring the closest pair of planes in the preceding lesson. In our fictitious race, the quadratic algorithm starts quite fast and is able to move quite a distance before it starts slowing down, similar to a runner that is getting tired and slowing down. The further it gets away from the start line, the slower it gets, although it never stops moving.

Not only do the algorithms progress through the race at different speeds, but also their way of moving varies from one type to another. We already mentioned that $O(n^2)$ solutions slow down as they progress along the race. How does this compare to the others?

Another type of runner taking part in our imaginary race is the linear algorithm. Linear algorithms are described with the notation of $O(n)$. Their speed on our race track is constant. Think of them as an old, reliable car moving at the same fixed speed.

In real life, solutions that have an $O(n)$ runtime complexity have a running performance that is directly proportional to the size of their input. This means, for example, that if you double the input size of a linear algorithm, the algorithm would also take about twice as long to finish.

The efficiency of each algorithm is always evaluated in the long run. *Given a big enough input, a linear algorithm will always perform better than a quadratic one.*

We can go much quicker than $O(n)$. Imagine that our algorithm is continually accelerating along the track instead of moving constantly. This is the opposite of quadratic runtime. Given enough distance, these solutions can get really fast. We say that these type of algorithms have a logarithmic complexity written as $O(\log n)$.

In real life, this means that the algorithm doesn't slow much as the size of the input increases. Again, it doesn't matter if at the start, the algorithm performs slower than a linear one for a small input. For a big enough input, a logarithmic solution will always outperform the linear one.

Can we go even faster? It turns out that there is another complexity class of algorithms that performs even better.

Picture a runner in our race who has the ability to teleport in constant time to any location along our infinite track. Even if the teleportation takes a long time, as long as it's constant and doesn't depend on the distance traveled, this type of runner will always beat any other. No matter how long the teleportation takes, given enough distance, the algorithm will always arrive there first. This is what is known as a constant runtime complexity, written as $O(1)$. Solutions that belong to this complexity class will have a runtime independent of the input size given.

On the other side of the spectrum, we can find algorithms that are much slower than quadratic ones. Complexities such as cubic with $O(n^3)$ or quartic with $O(n^4)$ are examples. All of the mentioned complexities up to this point are said to be polynomial complexities.

 NOTE   A polynomial is simply a mathematical term used for expressions. Expressions such as $3x^5 + 2x^3 + 6$, $2x - 3$, or even just 5 are all good examples. The key here is that polynomial complexities are of the form $O(n^k)$, where k is a positive, non-fractional constant.

Not all solutions have a polynomial time behavior. A particular class of algorithms scale really badly in proportion to their input with a runtime performance of $O(k^n)$. In this class, the efficiency degrades exponentially with the input size. All the other types of polynomial algorithms will outperform any exponential one pretty fast. **Figure 1.2** shows how this type of behavior compares with the previously mentioned polynomial algorithms. Figure 1.2 also shows how fast an exponential algorithm degrades with input size.

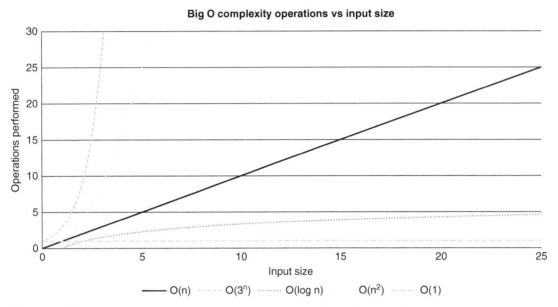

Figure 1.2   Operations performed versus input size for different algorithms

How much faster does a logarithmic algorithm perform versus a quadratic one? Let's try to pick a particular example. A specific algorithm performs about two operations to solve a problem; however, the relation to its input is $O(n^2)$.

Assuming each operation is a slow one (such as file access) and has a constant time of about 0.25 milliseconds, the time required to perform those operations will be as shown in **Table 1.3**. We work out the timings by $Time = 0.25 \,^*operations \,^* n^2$, where operations is the number of operations performed (in this example it's equal to 2), n is the input size, and 0.25 is the time taken per operation.

Table 1.3   How fast does it run?

Input Size (n)	Time: 2 Operations $O(n^2)$	Time: 400 Operations $O(\log n)$
10	50 milliseconds	100 milliseconds
100	5 seconds	200 milliseconds
1000	8.3 minutes	300 milliseconds
10000	13.8 hours	400 milliseconds

Our logarithmic algorithm performs around 400 operations; however, its relation to the input size is logarithmic. Although this algorithm is slower for a smaller input, it quickly overtakes the quadratic algorithm. You can notice that, with a large enough input, the difference in performance is huge. In this case, we work out the timing using $Time = 0.25 \,^*operations \,^* \log n$, with $operations = 400$.

Test yourself on this concept by completing Lab Activity 1.2.A: Developing a Timing Table Using the Exponential Algorithm.

In this lesson, we have compared different types of algorithmic runtime complexities. We have seen how each compares against the others, starting from the theory's fastest of $O(1)$ to some of the slowest with $O(k^n)$. It's also important to understand that there is a difference between theory and practice. For example, in real life, a quadratic algorithm may outperform a linear one if the operations performed are less, the input is a fixed size, and is small.

Lesson 1.2.3 Complexity Notation

In the previous lesson, we have seen how we can use the big O notation to measure the runtime performance to our algorithms in proportion to the input size. We have neither examined in detail what $O(n)$ really means nor have we considered the performance of our algorithm in relation to the type of input it's given.

Consider the following code in **Snippet 1.3**. The method accepts an array containing a string and searches for a match. If one is found, the index of the array is returned. We will use this example and try to measure the runtime complexity (see Snippet 1.3).

Snippet 1.3   Array search. Source class name: `ArraySearch`

```java
public int search(String strToMatch, String[] strArray) {
    for (int i = 0; i < strArray.length; i++) {
        if (strArray[i].equals(strToMatch)) {
            return i;
        }
    }
    return -1;
}
```

We have seen that for each processed item in the search array, we perform $5 + m$ operations, where m is the length of the search string. The next aspect to look at is to work out how often we perform this. The number of times we perform the operations mentioned in **Table 1.5** doesn't just rely on the length of our input; it also depends on how quick we are in finding our match in the input array, that is, it depends on the actual array's contents.

Table 1.5   Operations performed in the search method for every item

Operation Name	Code	Count
Array access	strArray[i]	1
String equality	.equals(strToMatch)	String length
Array pointer increment and assignment	i+i+1	2
Reading array length and comparing to pointer	i < strArray.length	2

 NOTE   The best case of an algorithm is when the input causes the algorithm to perform in the most efficient manner possible. The worst case is the opposite, which is when a particular input makes it behave in the least efficient manner possible.

If we are lucky and the item we are searching for is located in the first element of the search array, we perform only $5 + m$ operations. This is the best case and is the fastest manner our search can compute.

The worst case of this algorithm is either when our item is at the end of the array or when the item is not found at all. Both of these scenarios will have us then check the entire contents of the array. In the worst case, we end up performing $n(5 + m)$ operations, where n is the array size.

In this example, we can say that the worst-case runtime complexity for our algorithm is $O(mn)$ and our best case, when our algorithm finds a match immediately, is $O(m)$. We will see in the following lesson how we arrive at this result from $5 + m$ and $n(5 + m)$.

Another algorithmic analysis that is commonly used is the average case performance. The average case complexity can be found by averaging the performance over all possible inputs. This is useful, as in certain scenarios, the worst case has a low chance of occurring.

 NOTE Although we have the best, average, and worst-case complexities, the worst case is usually the most used when measuring and comparing different algorithms to one another.

Practice this concept by completing Practice Exercise 1.2: Identify the Best and Worst Performance of an Algorithm while Checking for Duplicates in an Array.

We have seen how we can analyze the number of operations performed in an algorithm and how we can use big O notation to describe the best and worst case. We also discussed how the notation can be used to describe any resource usage. In the next lesson, we'll describe some basic rules that are used when using the notation.

Lesson 1.2.4 Notation Rules

There are two simple rules to follow when we want to express an algorithm using the big O notation. In this lesson, we will understand how to convert the expression from $4n + 8n^2$ to the big O notation equivalent.

The first rule to follow is to drop any constants.

For example, $3n + 4$ becomes n and, a single constant such as 5 becomes 1. If an algorithm simply has 4 constant instructions that don't depend on the input, we say the algorithm is $O(1)$, also known as constant time complexity.

The second rule is to drop everything except the highest order.

Consider an algorithm that performs $n + n^2 + n^3$. The highest order variable of this is the n^3 part. If we keep the highest order, we end up with a big O runtime complexity of $O(n^3)$.

Test yourself on this concept by completing Lab Activity 1.2.B: Converting Expressions to Big O Notations Lab Exercise.

In this lesson, we have explored two simple rules used for converting expressions to big O notations. We have also learned why we keep only the highest order from the expression. In the next lesson, we shall see some examples of algorithms with different complexities.

LESSON 1.3 IDENTIFYING ALGORITHMS WITH DIFFERENT COMPLEXITIES

In this lesson, we shall look into examples of different complexities. This is important so that we can learn to recognize algorithms that belong to different complexity classes and possibly attempt improving the performance of each.

NOTE   Figuring out the worst case complexity can be quite difficult for some algorithms. Sometimes, this requires some experience and is best learned by looking at many examples and getting familiar with different types of algorithms.

Lesson 1.3.1 Linear Complexity

Linear algorithms are the ones where the work done varies in direct proportion with the input size, that is, if you double the input size, you double the work done. These typically involve a single pass through the input.

The problem presented in this example is that of counting the number of occurrences of a particular character in a string. Imagine we are given the string "Sally sells sea shells on the seashore," and we want to find out the number of occurrences of the letter "a."

The following code in **Snippet 1.5** goes through each character in the input string and if the character at the current position matches the search letter, a counter is increased. At the end of the loop, the final count is returned (see Snippet 1.5).

Snippet 1.5   Count the number of characters in a string. Source class name: `CountChars`

```
public int countChars(char c, String str) {
    int count = 0;
    for (int i = 0; i < str.length(); i++) {
        if (str.charAt(i) == c) count++;
    }
    return count;
}
```

Linear complexity algorithms are the most common types of algorithms. These usually make a single pass on the input and thus scale proportionally with the input size. In this lesson, we have seen one such example.

Lesson 1.3.2 Quadratic Complexity

Quadratic complexity algorithms are not very efficient for large input sizes. The work done increases following a quadratic proportion as we increase our input size. We already saw an example of a $O(n^2)$ in our minimum distance solution in Snippet 1.2. There are many other examples, such as bubble and selection sorting.

The problem presented in this example is about finding the common elements contained in two arrays (assuming no duplicate values exist in each array), producing the intersection of the two inputs. This results in a runtime complexity of $O(mn)$, where m and n are the sizes of the first and second input arrays. If the input arrays are the same size as n elements, this results in a runtime of $O(n^2)$. This can be demonstrated with the help of code:

Consider the method shown in **Snippet 1.6**. Can you figure out what the worst and best space time complexity is? For both cases, can you explain what is different in the inputs?

 NOTE   When calculating the space complexity, the memory consumed for the input arguments should be ignored. Only memory allocated inside the algorithms should be considered.

Snippet 1.6   Intersection between two arrays. Source class name: `SimpleIntersection`

```java
public List<Integer> intersection(int[] a, int[] b) {
    List<Integer> result = new ArrayList<>(a.length);
    for (int x : a) {
        for (int y : b) {
            if (x == y) result.add(x);
        }
    }
    return result;
}
```

The amount of memory we use is dictated by the size of our result listed in our method. The bigger this list, the more memory we're using.

The best case is when we use the least amount of memory. This is when the list is empty, that is, when we have no common elements between the two arrays. Thus, this method has a best case space complexity of $O(1)$, when there is no intersection.

The worst case is just the opposite, when we have all the elements in both arrays. This can happen when the arrays are equal to each other, although the numbers may be in a different order. The memory in this case is equal to the size of one of our input arrays. In short, the worst space complexity of the method is $O(n)$.

In this lesson, we have shown examples of quadratic algorithms. Many other examples exist. In the next lesson, we will also describe a poorly-performing sorting algorithm, which is $O(n^2)$, called bubble sort.

Lesson 1.3.3 Logarithmic Complexity

Logarithmic complexity algorithms are very fast, and their performance hardly degrades as you increase the problem size. These types of algorithm scale really well. Code that has a runtime complexity of $O(\log n)$ is usually recognizable since it systematically divides the input in several steps. Common examples that operate in logarithmic times are database indexes and binary trees. If we want to find an item in a list, we can do it much more efficiently if the input list is sorted in some specific order. We can then use this ordering by jumping to specific positions of our list and skipping over a number of elements.

Snippet 1.7 shows an implementation of the binary search in Java. The method uses three array pointers – a start, an end, and a midpoint. The algorithm starts by checking the middle element in the array. If the element is not found and is less than the value at the middle, we choose to search in the lower half; otherwise, we choose the upper half. **Figure 1.3** shows the steps involved when doing a binary search. See Snippet 1.7.

Snippet 1.7   Binary search. Source class name: `BinarySearch`

```java
public boolean binarySearch(int x, int[] sortedNumbers) {
    int end = sortedNumbers.length - 1;
    int start = 0;
    while (start <= end) {
        int mid = (end - start) / 2 + start;
        if (sortedNumbers[mid] == x) return true;
        else if (sortedNumbers[mid] > x) end = mid - 1;
        else start = mid + 1;
    }
    return false;
}
```

Take a look at Figure 1.3 diagram given in Figure 1.3.

Figure 1.3   Binary search steps

Assuming the worst-case scenario, how big would the input size have to be if our binary search algorithm is 95 array jumps (such as the one shown in Figure 1.3)?

Since this is a binary search, where we're splitting the search space in two, we should use a logarithm of base 2.

Also, the inverse of a logarithm is the exponential. Thus, we can say the following:

- $\log_2 n = 95$
- $2^{95} = n$
- $39614081257132168796771975168 = n$

 NOTE   For the record, 2^{95} is larger than the number of seconds in the universe by far. This example demonstrates how well these types of algorithm scale. Even for huge inputs, the number of steps performed stays very small.

Logarithmic algorithms are the opposite of exponential ones. As the input gets bigger, the rate of performance degradation gets smaller. This is a very desirable property as it means that our problem can scale to a huge size and would hardly affect our performance. In this lesson, we gave one such example of this class of complexity.

Lesson 1.3.4 Exponential Complexity

As we have seen previously, algorithms that have an exponential runtime complexity scale really poorly. There are many examples of problems for which only an $O(k^n)$ solution is known. Improving these algorithms is a very dynamic area of study in computer science. Examples of these include the traveling salesman problem and cracking a password using a brute force approach. Now, let's see an example of such problem.

A prime number is only divisible by itself and one. The example problem we present here is called the "prime factorization problem." It turns out that if you have the right set of prime numbers, you can create any other possible number by multiplying them all together. The problem is to find out these prime numbers. More specifically, given an integer input, find all the prime numbers that are factors of the input (primes that when multiplied together give us the input).

Snippet 1.8 shows one implementation for this problem, called "trail division." If we take an input decimal number of n digits, this algorithm would perform in $O(10^n)$ in the worst case. The algorithm works by using a counter (called factor in Snippet 1.8) starting at two and checks whether if it's a factor of the input. This check is done by using the modulus operator. If the modulus operation leaves no remainder, then the value of the counter is a factor and is added to the factor list. The input is then divided by this factor. If the counter is not a factor (the mod operation leaves a remainder), then the counter is incremented by one. This continues until x is reduced to one. This is demonstrated in Snippet 1.8.

Snippet 1.8   Prime factors. Source class name: `FindPrimeFactors`

```java
public List<Long> primeFactors(long x) {
    ArrayList<Long> result = new ArrayList<>();
    long factor = 2;
    while (x > 1) {
        if (x % factor == 0) {
            result.add(factor);
            x /= factor;
        } else {
            factor += 1;
        }
    }
    return result;
}
```

Try executing the preceding code for the following two numbers:

- 2100078578
- 2100078577

Why does it take so long when you try the second number? What type of input triggers the worst-case runtime of this code?

The worst case of the algorithm is when the input is a prime number, wherein it needs to sequentially count all the way up to the prime number. This is what happens in the second input.

On the other hand, the largest prime factor for the first input is only 10973, so the algorithm only needs to count up to this, which it can do quickly.

Exponential complexity algorithms are usually best avoided, and an alternate solution should be investigated. This is due to its really bad scaling with the input size. This is not to say that these types of algorithms are useless. They may be suitable if the input size is small enough or if it's guaranteed not to hit the worst case.

Lesson 1.3.5 Constant Complexity

The efficiency of constant runtime algorithms remains fixed as we increase the input size. Many examples of these exist. Consider, for example, accessing an element in an array. Access performance doesn't depend on the size of the array, so as we increase the size of the array, the access speed stays constant.

Consider the code in **Snippet 1.9**. The number of operations performed remains constant, irrespective of the size of the input radius. Such an algorithm is said to have a runtime complexity of $O(1)$ (see Snippet 1.9).

Snippet 1.9   Circle circumference. Source class name: `CircleOperations`

```
private double circleCircumference(int radius) {
    return 2.0 * Math.PI * radius;
}
```

Constant complexity algorithms are the most desirable out of all the complexity classes for the best scaling. Many of the simple mathematical functions, such as finding the distance between two points and mapping a three-dimensional coordinate to a two-dimensional one, all fall under this class.

Test yourself on this concept by completing Lab Activity 1.3: Developing a Faster Intersection Algorithm.

SUMMARY

In this module, we gave an introduction to algorithmic complexity and the notation to describe it. We have shown you how big O notation can be used to describe how well an algorithm scales as the input gets bigger. We have also seen various examples of complexities and shown you how you can intuitively differentiate between them. Understanding big O notations comes in handy when you need to design and implement new solutions or when you are diagnosing performance issues.

SORTING ALGORITHMS AND FUNDAMENTAL DATA STRUCTURES

MODULE OBJECTIVES

BY THE END OF THIS LESSON, YOU WILL BE ABLE TO:

1. Describe how bubble sorting works
2. Implement faster sorting with quicksort
3. Characterize merge sorting
4. Build a linked list data structure
5. Implement queues
6. Describe the stack data structure

INTRODUCTION

In the previous module, we saw how the intersection problem can be improved by using a sorting algorithm. This is common with many problems. If the data is organized in an ordered manner, a more efficient solution can be developed. In this lesson, we will start by exploring three types of sorting techniques, which are bubble, quick, and merge sorting. Later, we will learn different ways to organize data using fundamental data structures.

LESSON 2.1 INTRODUCING BUBBLE SORTING

Bubble sorting is the simplest sorting algorithm out there. The technique involves making multiple passes over the input array and swapping unordered elements close to one another. The technique is called bubble sort, as the sorted list "bubbles" up from the tail end of the list.

Lesson 2.1.1 Understanding Bubble Sorting

All sorting algorithms accept a list of elements and return them ordered. The main difference between each algorithm is the manner in which the sorting is done. Bubble sorting works by swapping adjacent elements. This pushes the sorted elements toward the end of the list.

Snippet 2.1 shows the pseudocode for bubble sort. The algorithm involves three simple tasks, which involves repeatedly stepping through the list to sort, comparing adjacent elements, and swapping them if the first element is bigger than the second.

Snippet 2.1   Bubble sort pseudocode

```
bubbleSort(array)
  n = length(array)
  for (k = 1 until n)
    for (j = 0 until -1)
      if(array[j] > array[j + 1])
        swap(array, j, j + 1)
```

How many passes do we need to perform on the array until our list is sorted? It turns out that to guarantee that our list is sorted, we need to do $(n - 1)$ passes on the list, n being the length of our array. We will show why $(n - 1)$ passes are needed in the next section, but this is the main reason why bubble sort has a runtime complexity of $O(n^2)$, since we're processing n elements for $n - 1$ times.

 NOTE   The swap function in the Snippet 2.1 switches the values of the two array pointers j and j+1 using a temporary variable.

Practice this concept by completing Practice Exercise 2.1.A: Implementing Bubble Sort.

Although bubble sort is very easy to implement, it's also one of the slowest sorting methods out there. In the next lesson, we will look at how we can slightly improve the performance of this algorithm.

Lesson 2.1.2 Improving Bubble Sorting

There are two main techniques we can adopt to improve the performance of bubble sort. It's important to realize that although both strategies improve the overall performance of bubble sort in the average case; in the worst case, the algorithm still has the same poor runtime complexity of $O(n^2)$.

The first small enhancement we can make to the original bubble sort is to make use of the fact that a sorted "bubble" is building at the end of the list. With every pass we make, another item is added to the bubble. This is the reason why $(n-1)$ passes are needed. This is also shown in **Figure 2.1**. In the figure, the items shown in the dotted circle are already sorted in the correct position.

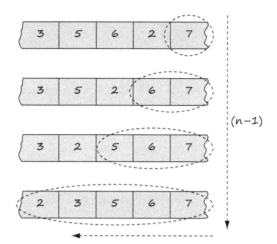

Figure 2.1   Bubble forming toward the end of the list

We can use this fact to avoid sorting elements inside this bubble. We can do this by slightly modifying our Java code, as shown in **Snippet 2.3**. In the inner loop, instead of processing until the end of the list, we can stop just before the sorted bubble, until `numbers.length - i`. For brevity, in Snippet 2.3, we have replaced the swap logic with a method.

Snippet 2.3   Bubble sort improvement 1. Source class name: `BubbleSort`

```
public void sortImprovement1(int[] numbers) {
    for (int i = 1; i < numbers.length; i++) {
        for (int j = 0; j < numbers.length - i; j++) {
            if (numbers[j] > numbers[j + 1]) {
                swap(numbers, j, j + 1);
            }
        }
    }
}
```

If we give a sorted list to our bubble sort algorithm, we will still make multiple passes on it without modifying it. We can further improve the algorithm by cutting short the outer loop when the list inside the array is fully sorted. We can check that the array is sorted by checking if any swaps were done during our last pass. In this manner, if we give our method an already sorted list, we just need to do one pass on the array and leave it untouched. This means that the best case is now $O(n)$, although the worst case stays the same.

Practice this concept by completing Practice Exercise 2.1.B: Improving Bubble Sorting.

Test yourself on this concept by completing Lab Activity 2.1: Implementing Selection Sort in Java.

In this lesson, we have seen some simple tricks on how to improve the bubble sort algorithm. In the following lessons, we shall look at some other sorting techniques that perform much faster than bubble sort.

> Test yourself on this concept by completing Lab Activity 2.1: Implementing Selection Sort in Java.

LESSON 2.2 UNDERSTANDING QUICKSORT

Quicksort is a big improvement over bubble sort. This sorting technique was developed by British computer scientist Tony Hoare. The algorithm works in three main steps:

1. Select a pivot.
2. Partition the list so that elements on the left of the pivot are less than the value of the pivot and the ones on the right are greater.
3. Repeat steps 1 and 2 on the left and right parts separately.

Since recursion is required for quicksort, we will begin this topic by giving an example of recursion. Later, we will see how the partitioning in the quicksort algorithm works, and in the end, we will put the recursion techniques to use.

Lesson 2.2.1 Understanding Recursion

Recursion is a useful tool for algorithm designers. It allows you to solve large problems by solving a smaller occurrence of the same problem.

Recursive functions usually have a common structure with the following components:

- One or more stopping conditions: Under certain conditions, it would stop the function from calling itself again
- One or more recursive calls: This is when a function (or method) calls itself

In the next example, we will pick the binary search problem seen in the previous module and change the algorithm to work in a recursive manner.

Consider the binary search problem discussed in Module 1, Algorithms and Complexities, listed in Snippet 1.7. The implementation is iterative, that is, it loops until an item is found or the end parameter is equal or greater than the start variable. The pseudocode in **Snippet 2.5** shows how we to change this method into a recursive function:

Snippet 2.5   Recursive binary search pseudocode

```
binarySearch(x, array, start, end)
  if(start <= end)
    mid = (end - start) / 2 + start
    if (array[mid] == x) return true
    if (array[mid] > x) return binarySearch(x, array, start, mid -
1)
    return binarySearch(x, array, mid + 1, end)
  return false
```

Practice this concept by completing Practice Exercise 2.2.A: Implementing Binary Search Recursively.

Recursion is an essential tool for any developer and we'll make use of it in many parts in this course. In this lesson, we implemented an example for binary searching. In the next lesson, we shall look at how partitioning works in the quicksort algorithm.

Lesson 2.2.2 Quicksort Partitioning

Partitioning is the process by which we reorder our array so that elements with a value less than our pivot are moved to the left of the pivot and those with a larger value are moved to the right (see **Figure 2.2**). There are numerous ways in which we can do this. Here, we will describe an easy-to-understand scheme known as Lomuto Partitioning.

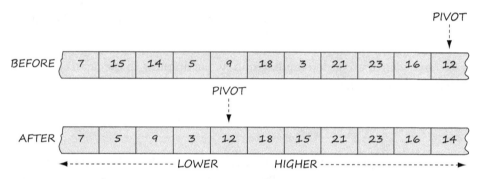

Figure 2.2   Before and after partitioning of an array

NOTE   Many other schemes exist. The Lomuto scheme has the drawback that it is not very efficient when it is used on already-sorted lists. The original Hoare partition scheme performs better and works by having the array processed from both ends.

To get a good perception on this partitioning scheme, it is best to simplify what the algorithm is doing in five simple steps, as follows:

1. Pick the right most element of the array as the pivot.
2. Start from the left and find the next element that is larger than the pivot.
3. Swap this element with the next, which is smaller than pivot element.
4. Repeat steps 2 and 3 until no more swapping is possible.
5. Swap the first item which is larger than the pivot's value with the pivot itself.

To perform efficient partitioning using the steps mentioned, we can make use of two pointers, one pointing to the first item larger than the pivot value and the other used to search for the value that is smaller than pivot value. In the code shown in **Snippet 2.7**, these are the integer pointers named x and i, respectively. The algorithm starts by choosing the pivot as the last item on the input array. It then processes the array from left to right in a single pass using the variable i. If the element currently being processed at i is smaller than the pivot, x is incremented and swapped. Using this technique, variable x is either pointing to a value larger than the pivot or the value of x is the same as i, in which case swapping will not modify the array. Once the loop exits, we perform the final step of swapping the first item that is larger than the pivot's value with the pivot. The code is shown in Snippet 2.7.

Snippet 2.7   Partitioning for quicksort. Source class name: `QuickSort`

```java
private int partition(int[] numbers, int start, int end) {
    int pivot = numbers[end];
    int x = start - 1;
    for (int i = start; i < end; i++) {
        if (numbers[i] < pivot) {
            x++;
            swap(numbers, x, i);
        }
    }
    swap(numbers, x + 1, end);
    return x + 1;
}
```

Test yourself on this concept by completing Lab Activity 2.2: Understanding the Partitioning Method.

In this lesson, we have gained an understanding of how partitioning in quicksort works. In the next lesson, we'll put the partitioning method to use by including it in the full quicksort algorithm.

Lesson 2.2.3 Putting It All Together

The quicksort is from a class of algorithms called divide and conquer. We will see many other examples from this class in the course, and we will go into detail on divide and conquer in Module 4, Algorithm Design Paradigms. For now, it's important to know that divide and conquer algorithms keep on splitting the problem into smaller ones until the problem is small enough that it becomes trivial to solve. This splitting can be easily implemented using recursion.

In quicksorting, we keep on recursively partitioning the array in this manner until the problem is small enough that we can easily solve it. When the array has only one element, the solution is simple: the array stays exactly as it is, as there is nothing to sort. This is the stopping condition of our recursive algorithm. When the array is larger than one element, we can keep dividing our array using the partitioning method we developed in the previous lesson.

 NOTE   There is also a non-recursive quicksort algorithm which makes use of a stack data structure, although it is a bit more complex to write. We will discuss stacks and lists later on in this lesson.

Snippet 2.8 shows the pseudocode for the complete quicksort. Just like most recursive functions, the code starts by checking the stopping condition. In this case, we check if the array has at least two elements by ensuring that the start array pointer is less than the end.

Snippet 2.8   Recursive quicksort pseudocode

```
quickSort(array, start, end)
  if(start < end)
    p = partition(array, start, end)
    quickSort(array, start, p - 1)
    quickSort(array, p + 1, end)
```

When we have at least two elements in the array, we call the partitioning method. Then, using the pivot's last position (returned by the partitioning method), we recursively quicksort the left part and then the right part. This is done by calling the same quicksort code using pointers of (start, p − 1) and (p + 1, end), not including the p, which is the pivot's position.

 NOTE   The trick to understanding how quicksort works is to realize that once we perform the partition call on the array, the element at the returned position (the pivot) doesn't need to move within the array anymore. This is because all the elements on its right are larger and the ones on the left are smaller, so the pivot is in the correct final position.

Practice this concept by completing Practice Exercise 2.2.B: Implementing QuickSort.

In this lesson, we have described the quicksort algorithm, which is much faster than the bubble sort algorithm that we saw in the previous section. On average, this algorithm performs in $O(n \log n)$, a huge improvement over bubble sort's $O(n^2)$. However, in the worst case, the algorithm still performs in $O(n^2)$. The worst-case input of quicksort depends on the type of partitioning scheme in use. In the Lomuto scheme discussed in this lesson, the worst case occurs when the input is already sorted. In the next lesson, we will examine another sorting algorithm for which the worst runtime case is $O(n \log n)$.

LESSON 2.3 USING MERGE SORT

Although the quicksort on average is pretty fast, it still has the theoretical worst time complexity of $O(n^2)$. In this lesson, we shall examine another sorting algorithm, called merge sort, in which the worst time complexity is $O(n \log n)$. Similar to quicksort, merge sort belongs to the divide and conquer class of algorithms. Merge sort can be summarized in three simple steps as follows:

1. Split the array in the middle.
2. Recursively sort each part separately.
3. Merge the two sorted parts together.

In the following lesson, we will develop the preceding steps gradually, at each turn slowly building our understanding of how merge sorting works.

 NOTE   Although merge sort is theoretically faster than quicksort, in practice, some implementations of quicksort can be more efficient than merge sort. Additionally, the merge sort uses about $O(n)$ memory as opposed to quicksort, which is $O(\log n)$.

Lesson 2.3.1 Dividing the Problem

In Lesson 2.2, we saw how we can use a recursive technique to split the problem into smaller multiple ones until the solution becomes easy to solve. Merge sort uses the same approach. The base case for our recursive technique is the same as quicksort. This is when the array is only one element long. When the array to sort only contains one item, the array is already sorted.

Figure 2.3 shows how merge sort array splitting occurs. At each step, we find the midpoint of the array and split the array into two. We then recursively sort the left and right part of the split array separately. We can stop the recursive call once the total elements to sort is equal to one as shown in the figure.

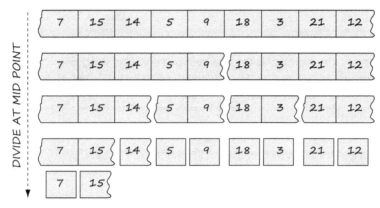

Figure 2.3   Showing the dividing steps for the merge sort algorithm

Practice this concept by completing Practice Exercise 2.3: Implementing Merge Sort.

The merge sort algorithm is from the same class of algorithms as quicksort; however, its runtime and space complexity are different. Instead of dividing the array from the pivot's position, the merge sort always partitions the array at the midpoint. This is a similar process to binary sort and results in $\log_2$ array divisions. In the next lesson, we will introduce the merge part of the merge sort algorithm, where the two different parts of the split array are combined into a sorted one.

Lesson 2.3.2 Merging the Problem

How do you merge two sorted lists into a sorted one? This is the task of the `merge()` function, which is found in **Snippet 2.12** later in this lesson. This process is shown in **Figure 2.4**. Merging two sorted lists is an easier task than sorting from scratch. This is similar to the intersection problem we saw in Module 1, Algorithms and Complexities. We can merge in linear time utilizing just two pointers and an empty array as shown in Figure 2.4.

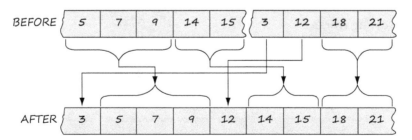

Figure 2.4   Before and after merging two sorted arrays

The pseudocode for the merging is shown in Snippet 2.12. In this code, the `copyArray()` function simply takes in a source array as a first argument and copies it to the target array, that is, the second argument. It makes use of the start variable as a pointer, indicating where to place the first element of the source array onto the target one.

Snippet 2.12   Merge pseudocode for the merge sort

```
merge(array, start, middle, end)
  i = start
  j = middle + 1
  arrayTemp = initArrayOfSize(end - start + 1)
  for (k = 0 until end-start)
    if (i <= middle && (j > end || array[i] <= array[j]))
      arrayTemp[k] = array[i]
      i++
    else
      arrayTemp[k] = array[j]
      j++
  copyArray(arrayTemp, array, start)
```

In the merging part of the merge sort, we create a temporary array which is of size equal to the size of two array parts together. We then do a single pass on this array, filling the temporary array one item at a time by picking the smallest item between the two input lists (represented by the start, middle, and end pointers). After picking an item from one of the lists, we advance the pointer of that list and repeat until the merge is complete.

Merge sort is theoretically one of the fastest sorting algorithms. The drawback of its speed is that it consumes a bit more memory, although some implementations exist that perform the merge step in place to save memory. For comparison, we present multiple sorting techniques with their runtime and memory performances in the following table:

Table 2.2   Sorting algorithms

Algorithm Name	Average Case	Worst Case	Memory	Stability
Bubble	$O(n^2)$	$O(n^2)$	$O(1)$	Stable
Selection	$O(n^2)$	$O(n^2)$	$O(1)$	Unstable
Insertion	$O(n^2)$	$O(n^2)$	$O(1)$	Stable
Quick	$O(n \log n)$	$O(n^2)$	$O(1)$	Unstable
Merge	$O(n \log n)$	$O(n \log n)$	$O(n)$	Stable
Heap	$O(n \log n)$	$O(n \log n)$	$O(1)$	Unstable

Test yourself on this concept by completing Lab Activity 2.3: Implementing Merge Sort in Java.

LESSON 2.4 GETTING STARTED WITH FUNDAMENTAL DATA STRUCTURES

Data structures are a way to organize data so that it is efficiently accessible for the problem you are trying to solve. Choosing the right data structure will depend on the type of problem you're trying to solve (dictating the manner you access your data), the amount of data you need to organize, and the medium you use to store your data (memory, disk, and so on).

We have already seen and used one example of a data structure. In the preceding lessons, we have made extensive use of arrays. Arrays are the most primitive of data structures. They provide access to your data using an index and are fixed in size (also called static). This is opposed to other dynamic data structures that can grow and make more space for data whenever it's needed.

Lesson 2.4.1 Introducing Data Structures

More formally, a data structure is an organization of data elements, a collection of functions that can be applied on the data (such as add, delete, and search) and any relations between the different data elements. The following table shows common operations that some data structures provide:

Table 2.3 Some Common Operations on Data Structures

Operation	Type	Description
search(key)	Non-modifying	An operation that, given the key to a particular value, will return the value stored in the data structure if it can be found.
size()	Non-modifying	The total number of values stored in the data structure.
add(value)	Modifying	Inserts a value in the data structure.
update(key, value)	Modifying	Updates an existing entry using the provided key and value.
delete(value)	Modifying	Removes an item of data from the data structure
minimum()	Non-modifying	An operation supported only by ordered data structures, which will return the value with the minimal key.
maximum()	Non-modifying	An operation supported only by ordered data structures, which will return the value with the maximum key.

In this lesson, we will see various types of dynamic data structures. We will start with linked lists, which are optimized for dynamic growth but are slow while searching. Then, we'll use these linked lists to implement other data structures on top, such as queues and stacks.

Lesson 2.4.2 Linked Lists Structure

A linked list is a list of data items where each item only knows about the next item in the list if there is one. **Figure 2.5** shows one such example. Each box in the figure represents a container for a data item we need to store. This container, called a node, contains our data values and a pointer to the next node in the list. As the figure shows, the node on the front of the list is called the head of the list and the last item of the list is called the tail. Separate pointers to these nodes are stored for easy access of the data structure.

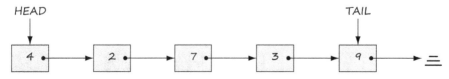

Figure 2.5 Linked List Example

The advantage of using a linked list as opposed to an array is that a linked list can grow dynamically. When using an array, you allocate space in the start and that space remains fixed. If you allocate too much and the space remains unused, you're wasting resources. On the other hand, if you make your array too small, the data might not fit. In a linked list, however, the space is not fixed. The structure grows dynamically as you add more data and it shrinks, freeing memory space as you remove it.

Using an object-oriented language, such as Java, let's model the linked list using separate node instances that are connected together to build our linked list. **Snippet 2.13** shows how we can model a linked list node in a Java class. The class contains a self-reference so we can link multiple nodes in list fashion, as shown in Figure 2.5.

Snippet 2.13 **Linked list node class, with getters and setters omitted for brevity. Source class name:** `Linkedlistnode`

```java
public class LinkedListNode<V> {
    private V value;
    private LinkedListNode<V> next;
    public LinkedListNode(V value, LinkedListNode<V> next) {
        this.value = value;
        this.next = next;
    }
    public Optional<LinkedListNode<V>> getNext() {
        return Optional.ofNullable(Next);
    }
}
```

Notice how we use Java's optional classes (instead of returning null pointers) to represent whether there is a link to the next node. The tail node of a linked list will always have an empty optional. We also make use of generics to model the type of data we want to store. This way, we can keep the structure as general as possible so that it can used by any data type.

 NOTE The `Optional` class was introduced in Java 8 to give the ability to represent optional values instead of using nulls.

Practice this concept by completing Practice Exercise 2.4.A: Converting the Linked List to a Doubly Linked List Structure.

In this lesson, we saw how to model a linked list node using classes, generics, and optional references. In the next lesson, we shall see how to implement some of the linked list operations.

Lesson 2.4.3 Linked Lists Operations

Before we can use any linked list operations, we need to initialize the data structure and mark it as empty. Conceptually, this is when the head of the list is pointing to nothing. We can do this in Java by adding this logic in a constructor. **Snippet 2.15** shows this. Notice that, once again, we use generics to hold the type of the items we want to store in the linked list:

Snippet 2.15 Initializing the linked list data structure using constructors. Source class name: `Linkedlist`

```java
public class LinkedList<V> {
    private LinkedListNode<V> head;
    public LinkedList() {
        head = null;
    }
}
```

How can we add and remove items from the head of the list? Adding a node in a linked list requires a two pointer reassignment. On the new node, you set the next pointer to point to whatever the head pointer is assigned to. Then, you set the head pointer to point to this newly created node. This process is shown in **Figure 2.6**. Deleting from the front of the list is the reverse. You set the head pointer to point to the next pointer of the node at the old head. For completeness, you can set this next pointer to point to nothing.

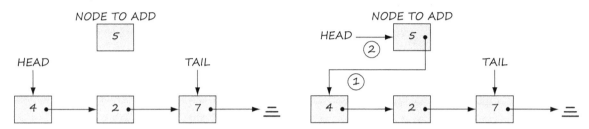

Figure 2.6   Adding a node to the front of the list

To locate an item in a list, we need to traverse the entire list until we find the item we're searching or reach the end of the list. This can be done easily by starting at the head pointer and always following the node's next pointer until you either find the node with the value you're looking for or you run out of nodes. For example, the next pointer is a null one.

Snippet 2.16 shows the addFront() and deleteFront() operations for a linked list. For the addFront() method, we simply create a new node with its next pointer set as the current head pointer. Then, we assign the head to the new node. Notice in the delete method how we make use of Java's Optional objects. If the head pointer is null, it will stay null and we don't change anything. Otherwise, we flatten it to the next pointer. Finally, we set the first node's next pointer as null. This last step is not necessary since the orphaned node will be garbage collected; however, we're including it for completeness.

Snippet 2.16   Adding and deleting from the front of the linked list. Source class name: `LinkedList`

```java
public void addFront(V item) {
    this.head = new LinkedListNode<>(item, head);
}
public void deleteFront() {
    Optional<LinkedListNode<V>> firstNode = Optional.
ofNullable(this.head);
    this.head = firstNode.flatMap(LinkedListNode::getNext).
orElse(null);
    firstNode.ifPresent(n -> n.setNext(null));
}
```

Snippet 2.17 shows one way to implement a find method. Again, observe how we make use of Java's Optional methods. We start a while loop from the head pointer and keep on moving to the next node as long as there is a node present and that node doesn't contain the item we're looking for. We then return the last pointer, which can be an empty optional or a node containing a match.

Snippet 2.17   Finding an item in a linked list. Source class name: `LinkedList`

```
public Optional<LinkedListNode<V>> find(V item) {
    Optional<LinkedListNode<V>> node = Optional.ofNullable(this.
head);
    while (node.filter(n -> n.getValue() != item).isPresent()) {
        node = node.flatMap(LinkedListNode::getNext);
    }
    return node;
}
```

In Snippet 2.16, we have shown how to add an item at the head of the list. How can we insert an item into a linked list at an arbitrary point? **Figure 2.7** shows how we can do this in two steps.

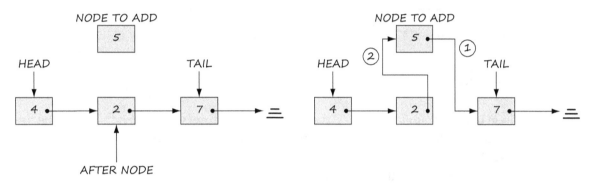

Figure 2.7   Adding a node at an arbitrary position in the list

Snippet 2.18 shows how we can do this. It is a Java method called `addAfter()` accepting a node and an item to insert. The method adds a node, containing the item, after the aNode argument. The implementation follows the steps shown in Figure 2.7.

Snippet 2.18   Solution method for `addAfter` operation. Source class name: `Linkedlist`

```
public void addAfter(LinkedListNode<V> aNode, V item) {
    aNode.setNext(new LinkedListNode<>(item, aNode.getNext().
orElse(null)));
}
```

Test yourself on this concept by completing Lab Activity 2.4.A: Traversing the Linked List.

In this lesson, we have seen how we can implement the various operations found in the linked list. The data structure will be a base tool that we will use to model queues and stacks. Linked lists will also be extensively used in more advanced algorithms further along the course.

Lesson 2.4.4 Queues

Queues are abstract data structures that are meant to emulate the workings of real life queues. They are used extensively in various applications, such resource allocation, scheduling, sorting, and many others. They are typically implemented using a doubly linked list, although many other implementations exists. A queue usually consists of two operations; an enqueue operation, where items are added to the rear of the queue, and an opposite dequeue operation, where items are removed from the front of the queue. These two operations make the mode of operation of this data structure First In First Out (FIFO).

We can implement an efficient queue using a doubly linked list. This enables us to implement the dequeue operation by removing an item from the head of the linked list. The enqueue operation is simply adding an item to the tail of the linked list. **Figure 2.8** shows how the two operations are performed.

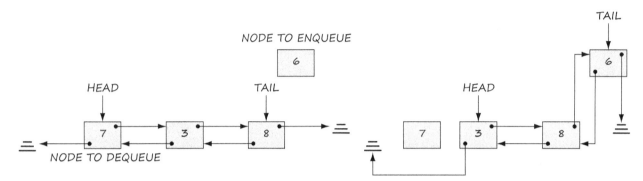

Figure 2.8   Enqueuing and dequeuing using a double linked list

To dequeue an item using a doubly linked list as a base data structure, we just need to move the head to the next item in the list and unlink the old head by pointing the previous pointer to nothing. Enqueuing at the tail is a three-step process. Point the new node's preceding pointer to the current tail, then point the current tail's next pointer to the new node, and finally moving the tail to the new node. The pseudocode for both of these operations is shown in the following code snippet:

Snippet 2.19   Enqueuing and dequeuing using a doubly linked list

```
dequeue(head)
  if (head != null)
    node = head
    head = head.next
    if (head != null) head.previous = null
    return node.value
  return null
enqueue(tail, item)
  node = new Node(item)
  node.previous = tail
  if (tail != null) tail.next = node
  if (head == null) head = node
  tail = node
```

Practice this concept by completing Practice Exercise 2.4.B: Adding and Deleting the Elements from the Queue.

Queues are dynamic data structures that have a FIFO ordering. In the next lesson, we shall explore another data structure with a different ordering called a stack.

Lesson 2.4.5 Stacks

Stacks, typically also implemented using linked lists, work differently than queues. Instead of the FIFO ordering, they have a Last In First Out (LIFO) ordering (see **Figure 2.9**). They have two main operations called push, which adds an item on top of the stack, and pop, which removes and returns one item from the top of the stack. Like queues, stacks are heavily used in many algorithms, such as depth first search traversal, expression evaluations, and many others.

Figure 2.9   Pushing and popping operations on a stack of papers

To model a stack, it's enough to use a simple linked list. The head of the linked list can be used to reference the top of the stack. Every time we need to push something on the top of our stack, we can use the addFront() method that we developed in the preceding lessons. The implementations differ only in the fact that the pop operation returns the optional item on the top of the stack. Both push and pop can been seen in the Java implementation in **Snippet 2.22**. Notice how the pop operation returns an optional value which is populated if the stack is not empty.

Snippet 2.22   Push and pop operations in java. Source class name: `Stack`

```java
public void push(V item) {
    head = new LinkedListNode<V>(item, head);
}


public Optional<V> pop() {
    Optional<LinkedListNode<V>> node = Optional.ofNullable(head);
    head = node.flatMap(LinkedListNode::getNext).orElse(null);
    return node.map(LinkedListNode::getValue);
}
```

 NOTE   A one-way linked list is enough to model a stack since we only need to operate from one end of the list. For a queue, we needed to modify both the head and tail of the linked list, hence it was more efficient to use a doubly linked list.

Practice this concept by completing Practice Exercise 2.4.C: Reversing a String.

Stack data structures are extensively used in computer science for many algorithms. In this section, we have seen how to implement them in a dynamic fashion using linked lists. In the next lesson, we shall see how to model stacks and queue in a static manner using arrays.

Lesson 2.4.6 Modeling Stacks and Queues Using Arrays

Stacks and queues don't necessarily need to be dynamic. You may want a more concise implementation if you know your data requirements are of a fixed size. Using an array approach to model stacks and queues guarantees that your data structure will only grow up to a certain size. The other advantage of using an array is that the array approach is more memory efficient if you can live with having a static data structure. The catch with static data structures is that the queue or stack can only grow to a maximum fixed size of your initially allocated array.

Implementing a stack using an array involves first initializing an empty array with a fixed size. Then, it's a matter of keeping an index pointer to the top of the stack, initially pointing to zero. As we push items on the stack, we place the item at this index and increment the pointer by one. When we need to pop an element, we reduce this pointer by one and read the value. This process is shown in **Snippet 2.24**.

Snippet 2.24   Stack using an array instead of linked list. Source class name: `Stackarray`

```java
public StackArray(int capacity) {
        array = (V[]) new Object[capacity];
}


    public void push(V item) {
        array[headPtr++] = item;
    }
    public Optional<V> pop() {
        if (headPtr > 0) return Optional.of(array[--headPtr]);
        else return Optional.empty();
    }
```

Implementing a queue using an array requires a little more thinking. The difficulty with a queue is that the structure is modified from both ends since it grows from the tail and shrinks from the head. As we enqueue and dequeue the contents of the queue, it seems to be moving toward the right of the array. We need to deal with what happens when the contents reaches the end of our array. To make the queue work in an array, we just need to let our data wrap around the edges (think PAC-MAN®, **Figure 2.10**).

Figure 2.10   Array wrap around analogy

When we reach the end of our array, we can just start again from the beginning index. This wrap around mechanism is called a circular buffer. It can be implemented using the modulus operator to access any element in the underlying array. **Snippet 2.25** shows how this works. Notice that when we enqueue an item, we place it at the tail position and increment the tail pointer using the mod operator. When the pointer is larger or equal to the size of the array, it wraps around and starts again from zero. The same happens on the dequeue method, where we access and increment the head pointer in a similar fashion. The code in Snippet 2.25 demonstrates this.

Snippet 2.25   Enqueue and dequeue using an array. Source class name: `QueueArray`

```java
public void enqueue(V item) {
    array[tailPtr] = item;
    tailPtr = (tailPtr + 1) % array.length;
}
public Optional<V> dequeue() {
    if (headPtr != tailPtr) {
        Optional<V> item = Optional.of(array[headPtr]);
        headPtr = (headPtr + 1) % array.length;
        return item;
    } else return Optional.empty();
}
```

> **NOTE**   The implementation in Snippet 2.25 does not check if the circular buffer is full before enqueuing another item.

Practice this concept by completing Practice Exercise 2.4.D: Safe Enqueing in an Array.

Test yourself on this concept by completing Lab Activity 2.4.B: Evaluating the Postfix Expression.

We have seen how both queues and stacks can be implemented using a static array structure instead of using the dynamic linked list. This has the advantage of consuming less memory per element as a linked list has to store pointers to other nodes. However, this comes at the cost of having a limit on the structure size.

SUMMARY

In this module, we laid the foundations for the more complex upcoming lessons. In the first few lessons, we saw how a simple problem such as sorting can have many solutions, all with different performance properties. We explored three main implementations, which were bubble, quick, and merge sort.

In later lessons, we introduced data structures and studied various implementations and use cases of linked lists, queues, and stacks. We also saw how some data structures can be used as building blocks to build more complex ones on top. In the next module, we will study hash tables and binary trees, two important and widely used data structures.

HASH TABLES AND BINARY SEARCH TREES

MODULE OBJECTIVES

BY THE END OF THIS MODULE, YOU WILL BE ABLE TO:

1. Describe how hash tables work
2. Implement two main techniques to deal with hash collisions
3. Characterize different hashing choices
4. Explain the terminology, structure, and operations of binary trees
5. Demonstrate various tree traversal techniques
6. Define balanced binary search trees

INTRODUCTION

In the preceding module, we introduced the concept of data structures by looking at arrays, linked lists, queues, and stacks. In this module, we will use some of these primitive structures to build more complex ones. We'll start the lesson by looking at hash tables, which are useful data structures for fast key-value lookup. In the second part of the module, we will learn about a more complex data structure that supports range queries, called binary trees.

LESSON 3.1 INTRODUCING HASH TABLES

A data structure that gives us the ability to insert, search, and optionally delete elements in a collection is called a data dictionary. Commonly, the type of data used is a key-value pair association, where we insert the key-value pair but search using a key to obtain the value.

Hash tables provide us with a fast data structure for organizing these key value pairs and implementing our data dictionary. They are useful in a wide variety of applications due to the quick lookup and ease of use for in-memory data storage. Insertion and search operations have a typical average runtime complexity of $O(1)$.

Lesson 3.1.1 Understanding Hash Tables

Let's look at an example problem to help us understand the need for hash tables. Imagine you are a teacher, instructing a class of a maximum capacity of 30 students. The students sit at their assigned desks every day. To make your life easier, you decide to assign a sequential number from 1 to 30 to each desk. You then use this number to identify each student, and use your self-developed app to bring up the student's records after you enter the desk number (see **Figure 3.1**). This way, you can quickly look up details such as the student's name, date of birth, notes, and exam history.

Figure 3.1   App for displaying student's records for student at desk number eight

In this problem, a simple array can be used to store all students' records in memory. Each of the array's positions can contain one student record. This would allow you to access the array directly using a strategy of *index = deskNumber − 1*. If, in a particular year you have fewer students, and not all the desks are occupied, you will place nulls at the corresponding array index. This solution is shown in **Figure 3.2**.

Figure 3.2   Example of direct addressing

This is an example of direct addressing, where each student's record is accessed using a key (the desk number). This type of solution can only be used when the possible key range is small enough to fit in an array which is directly in memory:

To help us determine how efficiently we are using memory, we can measure the load factor. The load factor is simply a metric showing how fully utilized our data structure is. When the class is at max capacity, all the elements in the array will contain a record. We say that the load factor of our data structure is 1 (or at 100%). If, for example, only 15 students out of the 30 spaces have registered for a particular year, the load factor is 0.5 (50%). A lower load factor value means that we are underutilizing and wasting memory.

Now, let's expand our example to include not just a class but an entire school, and instead of teaching one class, you have now been promoted to the head of the entire school. In this new position, you want to keep student records for every person currently enrolled. You also want to store historical records for any past students that are no longer in the school. You decide to use a unique 9-digit Student ID number.

Since our input range is quite big, directly addressing this would be very impractical. We can still store the students' records in an array sized to a few thousand. All we need to do is find a way to squeeze our input key range into our array index range. Essentially, this means mapping our nine-digit numeric passport into a four-digit one. This job can be done by what is known as a hash function. A hash function would accept a key (our passport number) and return an array index within the size of our array (see **Figure 3.3**). We say that a hash function maps our input key universe to our chosen hash range, which in this example is our array size.

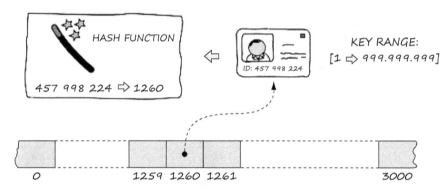

Figure 3.3   Using hash functions

Using a hash function enables us to use a much smaller array and saves us a lot of memory. However, there is a catch. Since we are forcing a bigger key space into a smaller one, there is a risk that multiple keys map to the same hashed array index. This is what is called a collision; we have a key hash to an already filled position. The strategy on how to deal with collisions together with the choice of hash function make up our hash table. **Snippet 3.1** shows a Java interface that defines our hash table API. We will gradually implement this interface in later sections of this lesson.

Snippet 3.1   Hashtable interface. Source class name: `Hashtable`

```
public interface HashTable<K,V> {
    void put(K key,V value);

    Optional<V> get(K key);

    void remove(K key);
}
```

In Java, the classes `java.util.Hashtable` and `java.util.HashMap` both implement the interface `HashTable`. The main difference between the two classes is that the `HashMap` is unsynchronized and permits nulls.

In this lesson, we first introduced direct addressing by looking at an example scenario. Later, we expanded the problem to a bigger key space, showing how hash tables can be used in such a scenario. In the next lesson, we will see two common solutions for dealing with hash table collisions.

Lesson 3.1.2 Dealing with Collisions with Chaining

What do we do when two keys hash to the same slot in our array? Overwriting the element in our array is not an option as this would mean losing records. One common solution to deal with collisions is a technique called chaining. In this solution, the hash table data is stored outside the actual array itself.

The idea behind chaining is that each entry in our hash array has a pointer to its own linked list. Any items we add to our hash table are stored in these linked lists. Initially, every entry in the array is initialized to contain an empty linked list. Whenever we insert a particular array slot in the hash table, we insert it at the head of the linked list associated with that position. In this way, we can support hash collisions. Another insert, on an already occupied array slot, would result in a new item at the head of its linked list. **Figure 3.4** shows an example in which two entries with different keys have hashed to the same array slot, resulting in the two records stored in the linked list.

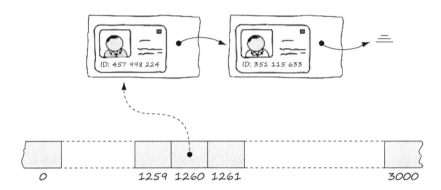

Figure 3.4   Using linked lists to chain multiple entries in one hash slot

Searching for a particular key requires first locating the array slot, and then traversing the linked list, one item at a time, looking for the required key until there is a match or the end of the list is reached. **Snippet 3.2** shows the search (`get`), insert (`put`), and delete (`remove`) operations. We make use of Java's linked list collection for this hash table implementation. In the constructor, the array is initialized with the given capacity, and each element is filled with an empty linked list.

Snippet 3.2   The chained hash table. Source class name: `ChainedHashTable`.

```java
public void put(K key, V value) {
    int hashValue = hashProvider.hashKey(key, array.length);
    array[hashValue].addFirst(new Pair<>(key, value));
}
public Optional<V> get(K key) {
    int hashValue = hashProvider.hashKey(key, array.length);
    return array[hashValue].stream()
            .filter(keyValue -> keyValue.getKey().equals(key))
            .findFirst()
            .map(Pair::getValue);
}
public void remove(K key) {
    int hashValue = hashProvider.hashKey(key, array.length);
    array[hashValue].removeIf(p -> p.getKey().equals(key));
}
```

Using the Java linked list collections enables us to use Java's lambda expressions when searching for the key in the `get(key)` method. When searching, we try to match the key with the ones found in the linked list and only return the optional value if a match is found. Using the lambda expressions also enables us to implement the delete operation in a clean manner by just calling the `removeif()` method with a key-matching predicate.

The `HashProvider` interface shown in **Snippet 3.2** simply provides us with a method that implements a hash function. We will implement this interface in the following lesson when we explore different hash techniques.

The runtime complexity for the chained hash table is dictated by how long our linked lists get. The best case is when every single item we insert in the hash table hashes to a different slot, that is, when there are no collisions. In the best case, we have a runtime of $O(1)$ when each linked list only contains one item, and we can directly access any item.

The worst case is the other extreme, when every single item hashes to the same value, resulting in a linked list with n items. When this happens, the performance degrades to $O(n)$ time to search for the required key. This is because we need to traverse the linked list of n nodes to search the required key.

This worst runtime complexity of $O(n)$ is applicable to all hash tables, not just chained ones. However, on average, and if the right hash function is chosen, the runtime performance of hash tables can be close to $O(1)$.

 NOTE A chained hash table has no load limit. Even in situations where none of the slots are empty, we can still add more items to the hash tables by continuing to append to the linked lists. This means that the load factor of a chained hash table can exceed the value of 1.

Chained hash tables are the most popular collision resolution implementation. The reason for this is that they are easy to implement, provide a good performance, and unlike some other techniques, allow the hash table structure to scale dynamically, and grow beyond the load factor of 1. In the next lesson, we will discuss another solution dealing with collisions, called open addressing.

Lesson 3.1.3 Dealing with Collisions with Open Addressing

In the previous lesson, we saw how we can deal with collisions using linked lists at each array position. A chained hash table will keep on growing without any load limit. Open addressing is just another way of tackling hash collisions. In open addressing, all items are stored in the array itself, making the structure static with a maximum load factor limit of 1. This means that once the array is full, you can't add any more items. The advantage of using open addressing is that, since you're not using linked lists, you're saving a bit of memory since you don't have to store any pointer references. You can then use this extra memory to have an even larger array and hold more of your key value pairs.

To insert in an open-addressed hash table, we hash the key and simply insert the item in the hash slot, the same as a normal hash table. If the slot is already occupied, we search for another empty slot and insert the item in it. The manner in which we search for another empty slot is called the **probe sequence**.

A simple strategy, shown in **Figure 3.5**, is to search by looking at the next available slot. This is called linear probing, where we start from the array index at the hash value and keep on increasing the index by one until we find an empty slot. The same probing technique needs to be used when searching for a key. We start from the hash slot and keep on advancing until we match the key or encounter an empty slot.

Figure 3.5   Linear probing in open addressing

Snippet 3.3 shows the pseudocode for linear probing insert. In this code, after we find the hash value we keep on increasing a pointer by one, searching for an empty slot. Once we reach the end of the array, we wrap around to the start using the modulus operator. This technique is similar to one we used when we implemented array-based stacks. We stop increasing the array pointer either when we find a null value (empty slot) or when we get back to where we started, meaning the hash table is full. Once we exit the loop, we store the key-value pair, but only if the hash table is not full.

The pseudocode is given in Snippet 3.3.

Snippet 3.3   Pseudocode for inserting using linear probing

```
insert(key, value, array)
  s = length(array)
  hashValue = hash(key, s)
  i = 0
  while (i < s and array[(hashValue + i) mod s] != null)
    i = i + 1
  if (i < s) array[(hashValue + i) mod s] = (key, value)
```

Searching for a key is similar to the insert operation. We first need to find the hash value from the key and then search the array in a linear fashion until we encounter the key, find a null value, or traverse the length of the array.

If we want to delete items from our open, addressed hash table, we cannot simply remove the entry from our array and mark it as null. If we did this, the search operation would not be able to check all possible array positions for which the key might have been found. This is because the search operation stops as soon as it finds a null.

One solution is to add a flag at each array position to signify that an item has been deleted without setting the entry to null. The search operation can then be modified to continue past entries marked as deleted. The insert operation also needs to be changed so that, if it encounters an entry marked as deleted, it writes the new item at that position.

Linear probing suffers from a problem called clustering. This occurs when a long succession of non-empty slots develop, degrading the search and insert performance. One way to improve this is to use a technique called quadratic probing. This strategy is similar to linear probing, except that we probe for the next empty slot using a quadratic formula of the form $h + (ai + bi^2)$, where h is the initial hash value, and a and b are constants. **Figure 3.6** shows the difference between using linear and quadratic probing. The diagram shows the order in which both techniques explore the array. In quadratic probing, we would change **Snippet 3.3** to check at array indexes of:

```
array[(hashValue + a*i + b*i^2) mod s]
```

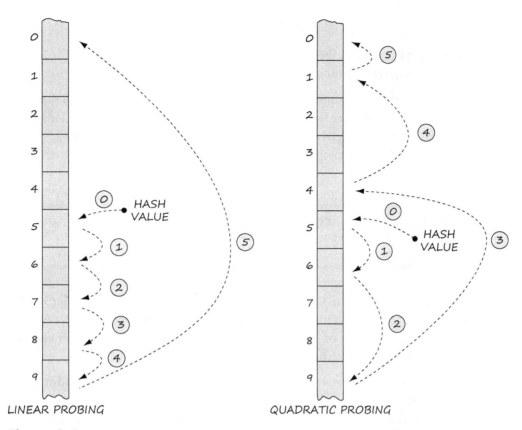

Figure 3.6   Linear versus quadratic probing

> **⚠ CAUTION**   Although quadratic probing reduces the effect of clustering, it suffers from a problem called secondary clustering. This is a milder form of clustering, however, it will still degrade performance. In addition, the constants a and b, and the array size need to be carefully chosen so that the probing explores the entire array.

One other probing strategy used in open-addressing hash tables is called double hashing. This makes use of another hash function to determine the step offset from the initial hash value. In double hashing, we probe the array using the expression $h+ih'(k)$, where h is the hash value and $h'(k)$ is a secondary hash function applied on the key. The probing mechanism is similar to linear probing, where we start with an i of zero and increase by one on every collision. Doing so results in probing the array every $h'(k)$ step. The advantage of double hashing is that the probing strategy changes on every key insert, reducing the chances of clustering.

In double hashing, care must be taken to ensure that the entire array is explored. This can be achieved using various tricks. For example, we can size our array to an even number and make sure the secondary hash function returns only odd numbers.

> Practice this concept by completing Practice Exercise 3.1.A: Carrying Out the Linear Probing Search Operation.

In this lesson, we have seen another manner for dealing with hash collisions by keeping all items in the array itself, saving memory, but limiting the structure statically. In the next lesson, we shall go into detail about some of the various hash functions available.

Lesson 3.1.4 Remainder and Multiplication Hash Functions

For hash tables, a hash function maps a specific key's space into a smaller number range. More formally, a hash function, f, maps keys of a specific data type to integers in a fixed interval $[0, ... , N-1]$. We say $f(x)$ hashes the value of x.

The hash function can accept only numeric data types. To allow us to use hash tables on more complex data types, we usually need to convert all these types into numeric representations. This translation varies, depending on the type of data. For example, a character can be changed into its UTF-8 (or ASCII) numeric equivalent. Converting a full string can be done by converting each character separately and then using a strategy to combine the characters into one value.

 NOTE   In Java, the `hashCode()` method converts an object into a numeric representation, which is ready to be used by a hash function. It is present in the object class and can be overridden using a custom implementation.

There are many techniques on how we can map keys from a wide range into smaller ones. An ideal hash function is one that reduces collisions to a minimum. In other words, when a good hash function is used, each key has the same probability of filling any of the slots in our array. In practice, finding an ideal hash function is very difficult unless we know the input distribution.

A simple technique to implement a hash function is what is known as the **remainder method**. The hash function simply takes in any numeric key, divides it by the table size (size of the array), and uses the resultant remainder as the hash value. This value can then be used as an index on the array. The codes in **Snippet 3.5** shows how the remainder hashing method can be implemented in Java using the modulus operator.

Snippet 3.5   The remainder method. Source class name: `RemainderHashing`

```java
public int hashKey(Integer key, int tableSize) {
    return key % tableSize;
}
```

The reminder method might result in many collisions if care is not taken when choosing an appropriate table size. Once again, consider the example given in the beginning of this lesson where we are using a unique Student ID number to identify a student in the school. To demonstrate the problem, we use an array-based hash table with a size of 1,000 elements.

A better choice of a table size is to use a prime number, ideally not too close to the power of 2. For example, the value of 1,447 is a good choice in our example, since it's not too close to 1,024 or 2,048 (2^{10} and 2^{11}) and is also prime. Using this value as a table size for our example would reduce collisions.

Using the remainder method restricts us on the choice of size for our hash table (to reduce the chance of collisions). To address this, we can use a different hashing technique, called the **multiplication method**. In this method, we multiply the key by a constant double value, k, in the range $0 < k < 1$. We then extract the fractional part from the result and multiply it by the size of our hash table. The hash value is then the floor of this result:

$$hash(x) = \lfloor s(xk \bmod 1) \rfloor$$

where

- k is a decimal in the range between 0 and 1
- s is the size of the hash table
- x is the key

> Practice this concept by completing Practice Exercise 3.1.B: Implementing the Multiplication Method for a Hash Table.

In this lesson, we have seen two basic techniques on how to compute hash values, the remainder method and the multiplication method. Both of these strategies are widely used in hash tables. In the next lesson, we will examine yet another mechanism, called universal hashing.

Lesson 3.1.5 Universal Hashing

Both the remainder and multiplication hashing methods have a common vulnerability. If an attacker knows the details of our hash function (table size and any constant values), he/she could devise an input key sequence resulting in a collision on every item, turning our hash table into a linked list and slowing down our program. To address this problem, a hashing technique called universal hashing can be used.

Universal hashing works by choosing a random function from a universal set of hash functions at the start of execution. This makes it difficult for an attacker to guess the exact workings of the hashing technique used. By using this technique, the same sequence of keys will produce a different sequence of hash values on every execution.

A set of hash functions, H, with size n, where each function maps a universe of keys U to a fixed range of $[0, s)$, is said to be **universal** for all pairs, where $a, b \in U$, $a \neq b$ and the probability that $h(a) = h(b)$, $h \in H$ is less than or equal to n/s.

In plain English, the preceding statement means that two keys have the chance of collision of $1/s$ when the hash function is selected at random from a universal set.

We can construct our set of universal hash functions by using two integer variables, i in a range of $[1, p)$, and j in a range of $[0, p)$, where p is a prime number larger than any possible value of the input key universe. We can then generate any hash function from this set using:

$$h_{ij}(x) = ((ix + j) \bmod p) \bmod s$$

where s is the size of the hash table and x is the key.

Snippet 3.7 shows a Java implementation of universal hashing suitable for integer-type keys. Note how our implementation makes use of the `BigInteger` class to work out the hash key. This is needed because multiplying a `long` Java numeric type with a large integer might result in a big enough value that exceeds the maximum capacity of a Java long. The choice of p in this method is such that any integer key input will always have a smaller value, since in Java an integer only has a maximum value of 2^{31}.

Snippet 3.7   Universal hashing for integer keys. Source class name: `UniversalHashing`

```java
public UniversalHashing() {
    j = BigInteger.valueOf((long) (Math.random() * p));
    i = BigInteger.valueOf(1 + (long) (Math.random() * (p -
1L)));
    }
    public int hashKey(Integer key, int tableSize) {
        return i.multiply(BigInteger.valueOf(key)).add(j)
                .mod(BigInteger.valueOf(p))
                .mod(BigInteger.valueOf(tableSize))
                .intValue();
    }
```

Java provides hash tables and built-in hashing mechanisms using the `Object. hashcode()` method. As a result of this, it is very difficult to implement a universal hashing table which integrates with Java's existing `hashcode()` method, since the `i` and `j` variables in the preceding code would have to be shared between different objects being inserted in the same table.

Universal hashing provides us with good results, minimizing collisions, and is immune to malicious attacks, since the function parameters are chosen at random.

> Test yourself on this concept by completing Lab Activity 3.1: Implementing Open Addressing.

LESSON 3.2 GETTING STARTED WITH BINARY SEARCH TREES

Like hash tables, binary search trees are fast lookup data structures for organizing key value pairs and implement the data dictionary operations. In addition to providing insert, search, and delete, binary tree supports efficient querying such as finding minimum and maximum, successor, and predecessor. When using balanced binary search trees, insert and search operations have a worst-case runtime complexity of $O(\log n)$. This is a big theoretical improvement over the worst-case scenario of a hash table, which is $O(n)$.

Lesson 3.2.1 Binary Tree Structure

The structure of a binary tree is composed of a series of nodes connected together via pointers. **Figure 3.7** shows the fundamental relation between nodes. Each node can have a maximum of two child nodes, a left one and a right one. Each node (except the top-level node) also has exactly one parent.

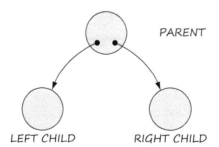

Figure 3.7 Showing a simple binary tree relation

Figure 3.8 shows some more terminology applied to binary trees. In this diagram, we also show that binary tree nodes can hold data items by showing the node storing different shapes. The top-level node is called the root node. The root node in a tree structure is the only node that doesn't have a parent. Nodes that don't have any children are called leaf nodes. The height of a tree is the number of hops it would take you to get from the root node to the furthest leaf node. The diagram shows an example of a tree which has a height of 2. The height of a tree is an important metric, as it affects the performance. The shallower a tree is (smaller height), the more efficient a tree structure is (see **Figure 3.9**).

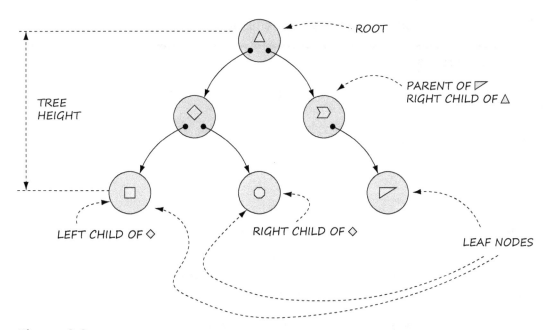

Figure 3.8   Binary tree terminology

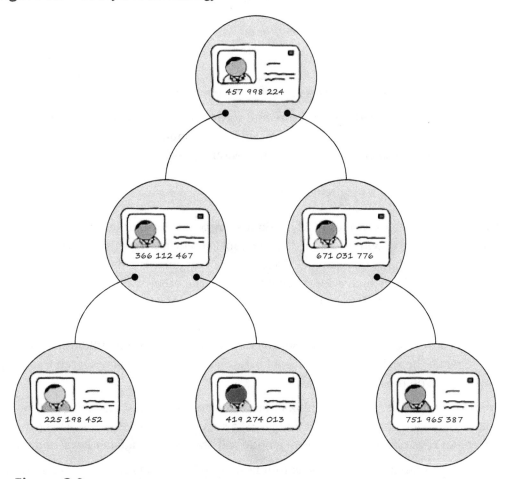

Figure 3.9   An example of a binary search tree

Similar to a linked list, the binary tree structure is modeled using pointers and node objects. In a linked list node, we only have a next pointer, referencing the next node in the list. Similarly, in a binary tree node we have two pointers, each one linking to one child. These are the left and right child pointers. The code in **Snippet 3.8** shows how we can model the binary tree node using a Java class.

Snippet 3.8 The binary tree node class. Some getters and setters have been omitted for brevity. Source class

```
name: BinaryTreeNode

public class BinaryTreeNode<K,V> {
    private BinaryTreeNode<K,V> left;
    private BinaryTreeNode<K,V> right;
    private K key;
    private V value;
    public BinaryTreeNode(K key, V value) {
        this.key = key;
        this.value = value;
    }
}
```

We can then have another class representing the binary tree itself, where the operations will be implemented. This class only needs to hold a pointer to the root node, since any node can be reached by starting from the root node and navigating down. In the code shown in **Snippet 3.9**, we show an interface declaring the binary tree.

Snippet 3.9 Binary tree interface. Source class name: `BinaryTree`

```
public interface BinaryTree<K,V> {
    void put(K key,V value);

    Optional<V> get(K key);
}
```

In this lesson, we have introduced the structure and terminology of binary trees. We then learned how to model each node using Java classes. In the next lesson, we will continue building on these concepts by introducing binary search trees and implementing the insert and search operations.

Lesson 3.2.2 Binary Search Tree Operations

Binary search trees are normal binary trees in which data is organized in an ordered manner. Consider the same problem we encountered in the previous lesson, of the school keeping a student's records by using the passport numbers as a key. **Figure 3.9** shows an example of how you can organize the data in a binary tree. Note how at each node the left child has a key which is less than its own. On the other hand, the right child has a larger key. Shown in the diagram, the root node has a left child containing a key of a smaller value than the root key. On the other hand, the right child has a key of a larger value than the root.

This rule is repeated through the entire tree. In a binary search tree, the left child will always have a smaller key than the parent, while the right child will have a larger one. Using this binary search tree property, we can create efficient operations on the tree structure.

As a result of this simple rule, the tree exhibits important properties. For example, note how all the nodes that are descendants of the left child of the root node have a smaller key than the root. This property is valid for any node of the tree. All keys on the left subtree of a node will always have smaller keys, and vice versa.

Searching in a binary search tree requires us to follow some simple instructions. We start at the root and at each node, we ask ourselves: "Is the key we're looking for equal to, less than, or greater than the key on this node?" If the key is equal, we're done and we have found our node. If the key is less, we follow the left child pointer, otherwise we follow the right one. We repeat this step until we find our key or hit a null child pointer.

The code in **Snippet 3.10** shows the search implementation. In this implementation, we use the power of recursion to perform the search. We start by checking if the tree is empty by checking whether the root is null.

If a root node is present, we compare the key and either return the value or recursively search the child nodes. To compare the key, we assume the provided key implements the comparable interface. Using Java's optional flat mapping makes our implementation much more concise.

Snippet 3.10   Binary search tree search operation. Source class name: `SimpleBinaryTree`

```java
public Optional<V> get(K key) {
    return Optional.ofNullable(root).flatMap(n -> get(key, n));
}


private Optional<V> get(K key, BinaryTreeNode<K, V> node) {
    if (((Comparable) key).compareTo(node.getKey()) == 0)
        return Optional.of(node.getValue());
    else if (((Comparable) key).compareTo(node.getKey()) < 0)
        return node.getLeft().flatMap(n -> get(key, n));
    else
        return node.getRight().flatMap(n -> get(key, n));
}
```

Java's `objectA.compareTo(objectB)` method in the comparable interface returns a negative integer, zero, or a positive integer if `objectA` is less than, equal to, or greater than `objectB`, respectively. Thus, the following statement:

```java
((Comparable) key).compareTo(node.getKey()) < 0
```

is conceptually the same as the following:

```java
key < node.getKey()
```

Inserting in a binary tree follows the same logic as the search operation. We start from the root and keep on looking for a location where we need to create a new node. This is shown in the code given in **Snippet 3.11**. Like the search operation, this Java implementation is also recursive. If the root node is absent we just create a new one, otherwise we recursively insert the key value pair each time by choosing the left or right child depending on the value of the key. We have three stopping conditions for the recursive call that are, as follows:

1. When the key is equal to the one on the node, we simply overwrite the entry.
2. When the left child is not present, we create a new node with the key value pair.
3. When the right child is not present, we create a new node with the key value pair.

Snippet 3.11   Binary search tree insert operation. Source class name: `SimpleBinaryTree`

```java
if (((Comparable) key).compareTo(node.getKey()) == 0) {
        node.setKey(key);
        node.setValue(value);
} else if (((Comparable) key).compareTo(node.getKey()) <0) {
        if (node.getLeft().isPresent())
            put(key, value, node.getLeft().get());
        else
            node.setLeft(new BinaryTreeNode<>(key, value));
} else {
        if (node.getRight().isPresent())
            put(key, value, node.getRight().get());
        else
            node.setRight(new BinaryTreeNode<>(key, value));
}
```

The code given in Snippet 3.11 demonstrates the binary search tree insert operation.

Binary tree deletion requires matching the subtree structure with a number of patterns and performing different actions with each case. In some situations, it requires that you connect the subtree with the parent of the deleted node, which can be quite complex.

> Practice this concept by completing Practice Exercise 3.2.A: Searching for a Minimum Key in a Binary Tree.

In this lesson, we have introduced binary search trees and explored how they can be used to organize key value pairs. We also saw how binary search trees can be used for simple range queries, such as finding the maximum and minimum keys. In the next lesson, we learn about all the different ways we can traverse a binary search tree.

Lesson 3.2.3 Traversing a Binary Search Tree

Traversing a binary tree is the process of stepping through each node of the tree and performing some sort of action on the data contained in the node (such as printing the key value pair). There are two main techniques to perform tree traversal: depth-first search and breadth-first search, more commonly known as DFS and BFS, respectively.

In DFS, the algorithm goes down a path of tree nodes until it cannot go any further. Once it cannot go further, it backtracks and discovers any remaining unexplored branches. A recursive implementation is shown in the code given in **Snippet 3.13**. In this traversal method, a different output sequence is produced depending on where the action is executed in the method.

Snippet 3.13   Depth-first search. Source class name: `SimpleBinaryTree`

```java
public void printDfs() {
    Optional.ofNullable(root).ifPresent(this::printDfs);
}

private void printDfs(BinaryTreeNode<K, V> node) {
    //System.out.println("PREORDER " + node.getKey());
    node.getLeft().ifPresent(this::printDfs);
    System.out.println("INORDER " + node.getKey());
    node.getRight().ifPresent(this::printDfs);
    //System.out.println("POSTORDER " + node.getKey());
}
```

In a **preorder** execution, we perform the action immediately, as soon as a new node is discovered. A **postorder** execution, on the other hand, is when both children of a node have been explored and we're about to backtrack. An **inorder** execution is done when the left child has been processed but before processing the right one. When using an inorder traversal, the keys in the binary search trees will be processed in ascending order.

In the breadth-first search traversal, the algorithm explores the binary tree one level at a time, left to right. The traversal starts from the root node and finishes at the leaf nodes. The output of an example binary tree is shown in **Figure 3.10**. To implement a BFS traversal of a binary tree, we can make use of a queue initialized to contain the root node. Then, while the queue is not empty, we read the first node on the queue, process it, and add first the left and then the right child to the queue.

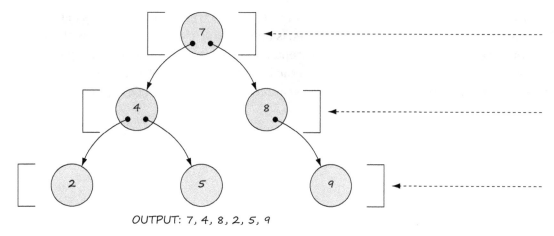

OUTPUT: 7, 4, 8, 2, 5, 9

Figure 3.10 Breadth-first search on a binary tree

We show the pseudocode of this as follows:

Snippet 3.14 Pseudocode for breadth-first search

```
breadthFirstSearch(root)
  if (root != null)
    queue = createQueue()
    enqueue(queue, root)
    while (not isEmpty(queue))
      node = dequeue(queue)
      process(node)
      if (node.left != null) enqueue(queue, node.left)
      if (node.right != null) enqueue(queue, node.right)
```

Test yourself on this concept by completing Lab Activity 3.2.A: Implementing BFS in Java.

In this lesson, we have learned about the various ways we can traverse a binary tree and the different ordering produced by each strategy. We have also seen how these algorithms can be implemented both in a recursive and in an iterative manner. In the next lesson, we will discuss a more restrictive type of binary search tree that ensures our data structure maintains a good performance, even in the worst input case.

Lesson 3.2.4 Balanced Binary Search Trees

The performance of a binary search tree is proportional to its height. This is because the search and insert operations start from the root and proceed down the tree one node at a time, doing a key comparison at each step. The taller the tree, the more steps are needed to accomplish this. Thus, if we determine the maximum possible height of a binary tree in relation to its input, we can find out the worst runtime complexity.

If we insert keys in a binary tree, by always adding on the right child of the parent node, we end up with a tree similar to the one shown on the left-hand side of **Figure 3.11**. In this diagram, only the right child pointers on each node are being used. We end up with a tree of height n, where n is the number of items added to our data structure. We get this kind of one-sided tree when the key input pattern is in order. In the example shown in Figure 3.11, we first insert **5** as a root, then **7** is added as the right child, the next is **12** as the next right child, and so on. Always inserting an increasing number results in the next node on the right. This one type of input pattern makes our binary search tree operations (search, insert, and delete) behave in the worst-case runtime of $O(n)$.

In Figure 3.11, on the right-hand side, we show another binary tree containing the same keys. This binary tree has been restructured with the effect that the tree is now shorter. Note that the tree is still valid, that is, the left child always has a key that is smaller than its parent, and vice versa. A balanced binary tree has a height of about $\log_2 n$. If we manage to find a way to rebalance the binary search tree at each insert in $O(\log n)$ or better, the worst-case runtime performance for inserts and searches would also be of $O(\log n)$.

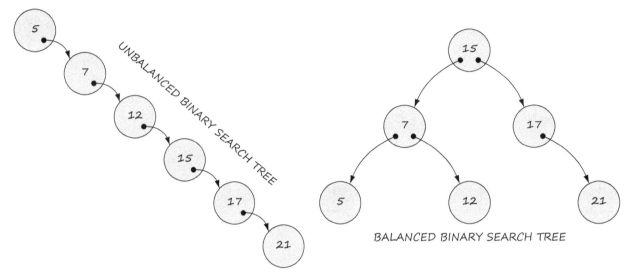

Figure 3.11   Unbalanced versus balanced binary trees

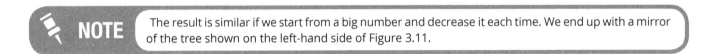

NOTE   The result is similar if we start from a big number and decrease it each time. We end up with a mirror of the tree shown on the left-hand side of Figure 3.11.

Luckily, various algorithms exist that self-balance the tree structure as you perform inserts. Some of the most common ones are as follows:

- AVL trees
- Red black trees
- AA trees

All of these algorithms check that the binary tree is following specific balancing rules at key insert. If, due to a new node being inserted, the tree becomes unbalanced, the self-balancing algorithm kicks in and restructures some of the nodes to keep the tree balanced. The technique to rebalance the nodes relies on tree rotations, where under certain conditions some of the parent and child nodes are rotated. Importantly, these modifications are also performed in the worst case of $O(\log n)$, meaning that both inserts and searches on binary trees have a worst runtime complexity of $O(\log n)$. In this lesson, we will examine tree rotations as they are the base operation for most self-balancing trees.

Figure 3.13 shows an example of a left and right rotation. Note how the node being rotated (node **5** in the right rotation and **9** in the left rotation) ends up being the new parent. Importantly, there is a constant number of child pointer reassignments. The properties of a binary search tree are still valid after a tree rotates, that is, a left child pointer always has a smaller key that points to its parent, and vice versa. This means that we can perform any number of these tree rotations and our binary search tree will still be valid.

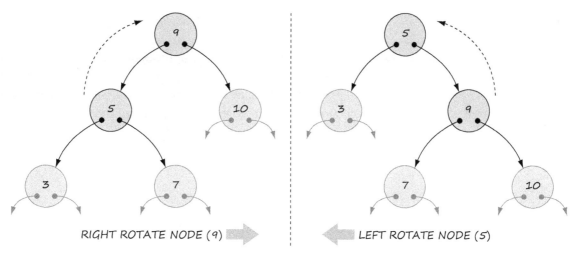

Figure 3.13   Left and right tree rotations

Snippet 3.15 shows how we perform a left rotation in Java. The method accepts a top-level node that needs rotation (node **5** in Figure 3.13) and its parent node. The method requires the parent node since it has to reassign its child pointer. Performing the opposite right rotation on the tree node is the mirror image of the method shown in Snippet 3.15.

Snippet 3.15   Java implementation of the left tree rotation. Source class name: `SimpleBinaryTree`

```
public void leftRotate(BinaryTreeNode<K, V> nodeX,
                       BinaryTreeNode<K, V> parent) {
   BinaryTreeNode<K, V> nodeY = nodeX.getRight().get();
   nodeX.setRight(nodeY.getLeft().orElse(null));
   if (parent == null)
       this.root = nodeY;
   else if (parent.getLeft().filter(n -> n == nodeX).isPresent())
       parent.setLeft(nodeY);
   else
       parent.setRight(nodeY);
   nodeY.setLeft(nodeX);
}
```

Practice this concept by completing Practice Exercise 3.2.B: Applying Right Tree Rotation.

The right rotation is an exact mirror image of the left rotation. It's enough to change all the left references with right references and vice versa.

In this lesson, we saw how we can improve the performance of binary search trees by using tree rotations to balance the data structure. This enables the tree to remain of a shorter height with a runtime complexity of $O(\log n)$.

Test yourself on this concept by completing Lab Activity 3.2.B: Retrieving the Successor of an Element When the Tree is Traversed in Inorder.

SUMMARY

In this module, we have studied two of the most commonly used data structures for implementing the data dictionary operation. Hash tables provide fast in-memory insertion and lookup operations. In addition, binary trees also give us the ability to perform various range queries, such as successor, predecessor, minimum, and maximum. In this module, we have seen examples of both data structures, and implementations of these operations.

ALGORITHM DESIGN PARADIGMS

MODULE OBJECTIVES

BY THE END OF THIS MODULE, YOU WILL BE ABLE TO:

1. Describe greedy, divide and conquer, and dynamic programming algorithm paradigms
2. Analyze common problems solved by using the described paradigms
3. List the properties of a problem to be solved by each paradigm
4. Solve some well-known problems that explain the applicability of each paradigm

INTRODUCTION

In the last module, we learned about hash tables and binary search trees. Today, we will start with the algorithm design paradigms. These design patterns can be seen as the generic methods or approaches that motivate the design of a class of algorithms.

Just as an algorithm is a higher abstraction than a computer program, an algorithm design paradigm is an abstraction higher than an algorithm. The choice of an algorithm paradigm is an important one when designing an algorithm.

This module will focus on the following three algorithm paradigms:

- Greedy
- Divide and conquer
- Dynamic programming

By becoming familiar with these higher abstractions, you can make more informed decisions when designing algorithms.

There are obviously more algorithm design paradigms, but these three already cover a broad range of problems. Some other paradigms we're not talking about in this course are backtracking and prune and search.

There are even paradigms focused on specific branches of computer science. The sweep line algorithms, in computational geometry, is an example of this.

LESSON 4.1 INTRODUCING GREEDY ALGORITHMS

Algorithms typically go through a sequence of steps, wherein each step you have a set of choices. Greedy algorithms, as the name suggests, follow the heuristic of making the locally optimum choice at each step, with the hope of arriving at a global optimum. To better understand what we mean by this, let's introduce a problem.

Lesson 4.1.1 The Activity Selection Problem

Peter is an energetic guy, and usually has many things to do in a given day. However, with the amount of things he wants to do, he is usually unable to do them all in a single day. What he usually does after waking up is write up a list of activities that he has to do, along with their time span. Then, looking at that list, he devises a plan for the day, trying to accommodate as many activities as possible.

Being an energetic guy, he usually rushes through this process and finds himself doing fewer activities than possible throughout the day. Can you help him maximize the amount of activities he can do in a day, given his schedule? An example of a schedule for Peter is given in **Table 4.1**.

Table 4.1 Peter's schedule

ID	Activity	Time Span
1	Tidy up his room	10:00–12:00
2	Going to the rock concert	20:00–23:00
3	Play chess at the local club	17:00–19:00
4	Take a shower	10:00–10:30
5	Dinner with friends	19:00–20:30
6	Play Civilization VI	21:30–23:00
7	Have lunch with girlfriend	12:30–13:30
8	Go to the cinema	20:00–22:00
9	Go biking in the park	17:00–19:30
10	Go to the beach	16:00–19:00
11	Go to the library	15:00–17:00

This is known as the activity selection problem. The problem is to schedule several competing activities that require exclusive use of a common resource (which is Peter, in this case), with the goal of selecting a maximum size set of activities that are mutually compatible.

In other words, we are trying to find the biggest set of activities that Peter can perform in a day. Each activity (a_i) has a start time (s_i) and a finish time (f_i). Two activities, a_i and a_j, are considered compatible if the intervals $[s_i, f_i)$ and $[s_j, f_j)$ do not overlap, for example, $s_i \geq f_j$ or $s_j \geq f_i$.

Looking at Peter's schedule, and converting the start and finish times to minutes since the start of a day, we can arrive at the times given in **Table 4.2**. To convert the times to minutes since the start of the day, we multiply the hours by 60 and add the minutes. For example, *activity 1* runs from 10:00 to 12:00. 10:00 is 600 (10*60 + 0) minutes since the start of the day, and 12:00 is 720 (12*60 + 0) minutes since the start of the day:

Table 4.2   Start and finish times of Peter's activities

a_i	1	2	3	4	5	6	7	8	9	10	11
s_i	600	1200	1020	600	1140	1290	750	1200	1020	960	900
f_i	720	1380	1140	630	1230	1380	810	1320	1170	1140	1020

For this example, the subset $\{a_1, a_3, a_5, a_6\}$ consists of mutually compatible activities, as their times don't overlap. It is not a maximum subset (i.e., we can find a set with a larger number of activities), since the subset $\{a_3, a_4, a_5, a_6, a_7, a_{11}\}$ is larger (note that the order of the activities is a_4, a_7, a_{11}, a_3, a_5 and a_6). In fact, it is a larger subset of mutually compatible activities. It is not the only one; another possible larger subset is $\{a_1, a_7, a_{11}, a_3, a_5, a_6\}$.

How should we approach this problem to find the maximum size set of activities that are mutually compatible? It turns out we should do the greedy choice. What this means is that, at each step of the algorithm, from the set of activities that we can still perform, we should choose one greedily.

The greedy choice may not be immediate, but you can intuitively think that we should select activities that leave Peter available for as many other activities as possible. Hence, from the set of activities that we are able to choose, we must choose the first one to finish, as that is the activity that would leave Peter available for as many of the activities that follow it as possible. If we sort activities by finish time, we can then always select the first activity we find that is compatible with the last activity selected for Peter.

> Practice this concept by completing Practice Exercise 4.1.A: Solving the Activity Selection Problem.

After having sorted the activities by finish time, the selection part of the algorithm runs in $O(n)$ time. Since we can't sort in $O(n)$, the overall complexity of this algorithm is bounded by the complexity of the sorting algorithm. As seen in previous lessons, we can sort in $O(n\log(n))$ so that's the runtime complexity of the algorithm we've devised for the activity selection problem. The algorithm looks good, but how can we be sure that it always arrives at the optimal solution?

Lesson 4.1.2 Ingredients of a Greedy Algorithm

There are two basic ingredients every greedy algorithm has in common. They are as follows:

- Optimal substructure property
- Greedy choice property

OPTIMAL SUBSTRUCTURE PROPERTY

The first step in solving an optimization problem by using a greedy approach is to characterize the structure of an optimal solution. A problem exhibits the optimal substructure property if an optimal solution to the problem within it contains optimal solutions to subproblems.

Intuitively, we can think that the activity selection problem exhibits the optimal substructure property in the sense that, if we suppose that a given activity belongs to a maximum size set of mutually compatible activities, then we are left to choose the maximum size set of mutually compatible activities from the ones that finish before this activity starts and that start after this activity finishes. Those two sets must also be maximum sets for the compatible activities, so that they can showcase the optimal substructure of this problem.

Formally, it is possible to prove that the activity selection problem exhibits optimal substructure. Let's assume we have the set of activities sorted in monotonically increasing order of finish time so that the following can be true for activities i and j:

$f_i \leq f_j$ if $i \leq j$

whereas f_i is denoting the finish time of activity i.

Suppose we denote by S_{ij}; the set of activities that start after activity a_i finish, and they finish before activity a_j starts. Thus, we wish to find a maximum set of mutually compatible activities in S_{ij}.

Let's say that the set is A_{ij}, and includes activity a_k. By including a_k in an optimal solution, we are left with two subproblems that are finding the maximum subset of mutually compatible activities in the set S_{ik} and set S_{kj}, which can be represented as follows:

$A_{ij} = A_{ik} U \{a_k\} U A_{kj}$.

Thus, the size of the maximum size set of mutually compatible activities in S_{ij} is given by the following:

$|A_{ij}| = |A_{ik}| + |A_{kj}| + 1.$

If we could find a set $A'kj$ of mutually compatible activities in S_{kj} where $|A'_{kj}| > |A_{kj}|$, then we could use A'_{kj} instead of A_{kj} in the optimal solution to the subproblem for S_{ij}. But that way, we would have something that contradicts the assumption that A_{ij} is an optimal solution:

$|A_{ik}| + |A'_{kj}| + 1 > |A_{ik}| + |A_{kj}| + 1 = |A_{ij}|$

GREEDY CHOICE PROPERTY

When searching for a possible solution to a problem, we usually consider various solutions, which we call the solution space.

When trying to find the best solution to a problem, we're usually interested in a global optimum, that is, the optimal solution from the whole set of possible solutions.

However, the solution space can exhibit other optimums. Namely, we can have local optimums, which are optimal solutions in a small neighborhood of possible solutions.

The greedy choice property states that from a local optimum we can reach a global optimum, without having to reconsider decisions that have already been made.

In the activity selection problem for Peter, we applied the greedy choice by always choosing the activity with the earliest finish time from the set of available activities.

Intuitively, we can think that this problem exhibits the greedy choice property in the sense that if we have a maximum size subset and we replace the activity from that set with the earliest finish time with one that finishes even earlier, we are always left with a maximum size set, making it safe to always choose the one with the earliest finish time.

It is possible to prove that the greedy choice is always part of some optimal solution.

Let's try to prove that, for any nonempty subproblem S_k, if a_m is an activity in S_k with the earliest finish time, then a_m is included in some maximum size subset of mutually compatible activities of S_k.

To prove it, let's assume the following:

- A_k is a maximum size subset of mutually compatible activities in S_k
- a_j is the activity in A_k with the earliest finish time

If $a_j = a_m$, we are done. If $a_j != a_m$, we can try to replace a_j by a_m in A_k, producing the set $A'_k = A_k - \{a_k\} U \{a_m\}$.

We can safely do that since the activities in A_k are disjoined. a_j is the first activity to finish in A_k, and $f_m <= f_j$.

Since $|A'_k| = |A_k|$, we conclude that A'_k is a maximum size subset of mutually compatible activities of S_k, and that it includes a_m.

Intuition usually helps us to decide whether a greedy algorithm produces the optimal solution, without having to formally prove the optimal substructure and the greedy choice properties. We're also going to cover a different paradigm of algorithm design in this lesson, which is dynamic programming that also requires problems to exhibit the optimal substructure property. If you are not sure if a greedy algorithm works for a given problem due to the greedy choice, you can always build a dynamic programming solution for it to gain some insight.

Lesson 4.1.3 Huffman Coding

To gain more insight about greedy algorithms, let's look at another problem that is solvable by a greedy algorithm.

Huffman codes represent a way of compressing data effectively. Data is considered to be a sequence of characters. Huffman's greedy algorithm uses a table with the frequency of each character to build up an optimal way of representing each character as a binary string.

To illustrate this, imagine we have a 100,000 character data file that we wish to store in a compressed fashion. The frequency of each character in the data file is given in **Table 4.3**.

Table 4.3   Frequency of each character in a data file

Character	a	b	c	d	e	f
Frequency	45000	13000	12000	16000	9000	5000

There are various ways to represent this information. For the purpose of this problem, let's say that we want to design a binary character code in which each character is represented by a unique binary string (which we shall call a "code word"). One option is to use a fixed-length code (e.g., each character is represented by a code word of the same size). If we opt for that, we need three bits to represent each the six characters, as shown in **Table 4.4**.

Table 4.4   Code word for each character

Character	a	b	c	d	e	f
Frequency	45000	13000	12000	16000	9000	5000
Code Word	000	001	010	011	100	101

Using this method, we need 300,000 bits to code the entire sequence of characters. Can we do better?

A variable-length code can do a lot better than a fixed-length code. Since we want to minimize the size of the compressed sequence of bits, we want to give short code words to frequent characters and long code words to infrequent characters. A possible code for this character sequence is shown in **Table 4.5**.

Table 4.5   Possible code for character sequence

Character	a	b	c	d	e	f
Frequency	45000	13000	12000	16000	9000	5000
Code Word	0	101	100	111	1101	1100

Instead of 300,000 bits, this code requires only 224,000 bits to represent the character sequence. Using this code, we save around 28% of space. The code we have presented is also an optimal character code for this sequence, as we shall see.

Lesson 4.1.4 Building a Huffman Code

Before we start studying an algorithm to solve this problem, we should introduce something called "prefix codes." Prefix codes are codes in which no code word is also a prefix of some other code word. As you have seen from the proposed variable length code, we must make sure that no code word is also a prefix of some other code word, since we want to concatenate on code words and unambiguously be able to decode it afterwards.

For example, using the code shown previously, we encode the string *abc* as *0101100*. Since no code word is a prefix of any other, decoding is vastly simplified, as we can identify the initial code word, translate it, and repeat the process on the remainder of the encoded sequence.

A convenient (for decoding purposes) representation of prefix codes is a binary tree whose leaves are the characters of the original data sequence. For the proposed variable-length code, we have the binary tree shown in **Figure 4.1**.

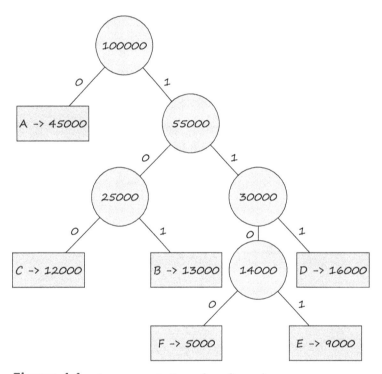

Figure 4.1   A representation of prefix codes

The binary code word for a character is the path from the root to that character, following in the binary digits in each edge. Note that each node also holds the frequency of characters under its subtree. Such a tree also has some interesting properties. A tree for an optimal prefix code has exactly $|C|$ leaves, C being the alphabet from which the characters are drawn. The number of internal nodes is exactly $|C| - 1$. We also know that the number of bits necessary to encode a particular character in a sequence is equal to the frequency of that character multiplied by the depth of the leaf that holds the character. As such, the number of bits required to encode the full character sequence is simply the sum of these values for all the characters in the alphabet.

If we can build such a tree, we can compute an optimal prefix code. David A. Huffman invented a greedy algorithm to construct an optimal prefix code, called a **Huffman Code**. Its basic idea is to build the tree in a bottom-up fashion. We start with just the leaf, one for each character. We then repeatedly join the two least-frequent nodes, until we are left with a single node, which is the root of the tree.

> Practice this concept by completing Practice Exercise 4.1.B: Developing an Algorithm to Generate Code Words Using Huffman Coding.

We make use of a priority queue to store our nodes, making it very efficient ($O(\log n)$) to extract the node with the least frequency. A priority queue is like a queue, or a stack, but each element has an additional "priority" associated with it. An element with a higher priority is served before an element with lower priority. Priority queues are usually implemented using heaps, which usually provide $O(1)$ time to find the element with a higher priority, $O(\log n)$ to insert an element, and $O(\log n)$ time to remove the element with a higher priority.

To analyze the running time of Huffman's algorithm, let's break it down into steps. We first go through each character in the frequencies map and build a node that we later insert in the priority queue. It takes $O(\log n)$ time to insert a node in the priority queue. Since we go through each character, it takes $O(n\log n)$ to create and initially populate the priority queue. The second for loop executes exactly $n-1$ times. Each time, we perform two removes from the priority queue, each one taking $O(\log n)$ time. In its whole, the for loop takes $O(n\log n)$ time. We thus have two steps, each taking $O(n\log n)$ time, which leaves us at a total running time on a set of n characters of $O(n\log n)$.

> Test yourself on this concept by completing Lab Activity 4.1: Implementing a Greedy Algorithm to Compute Egyptian Fractions.

We introduced the greedy paradigm of algorithm design using the activity selection problem as a running example. We introduced the two properties a problem must observe to be optimally solved by a greedy algorithm: optimal substructure and greedy choice. To gain intuition about the applicability of greedy algorithms, we later explored two other problems that are solvable by a greedy approach: Huffman coding and Egyptian fractions.

LESSON 4.2 GETTING STARTED WITH DIVIDE AND CONQUER ALGORITHMS

In the previous module, we introduced, among other sorting algorithms, merge and quicksort. A peculiarity of both algorithms is that they divide the problem into subproblems that are smaller instances of the same, solve each one of the subproblems recursively, and then combine the solutions to the subproblems into the solution for the original problem. This strategy forms the basis of the divide and conquer paradigm.

Lesson 4.2.1 The Divide and Conquer Approach

In a divide and conquer approach, we solve a problem recursively, applying the following three steps at each level of recursion:

- **Divide** the problem into more than one subproblems that are smaller instances of the same problem.
- **Conquer** the subproblems by solving them recursively. Eventually, the subproblem sizes are small enough for them to be solved in a straightforward manner.
- **Combine** the solutions to the subproblems in the solution for the original problem.

When a subproblem is large enough to be solved recursively, we call that the **recursive case**. When a subproblem becomes small enough that recursion is no longer necessary, we say that we have reached to the **base case**. It is common to solve subproblems that are different from the original problem, in addition to the subproblems that are smaller instances of the main problem. Solving these problems is considered to be part of the combine step.

In Module 2, Sorting Algorithms and Fundamental Data Structures, we saw that the runtime complexity of merge sort was $O(n\log n)$. We can also see that the worst-case running time $T(n)$ of merge sort can be described by the following recurrence:

$$T(n) = \begin{cases} O(1) & \text{if } n = 1, \\ 2T(n/2) + O(n) & \text{if } n > 1. \end{cases}$$

These kinds of recurrences arise frequently and characterize divide and conquer algorithms. If we generalize the recursion to the following:

$$T(n) = \begin{cases} O(1) & \text{if } n = 1, \\ aT(n/b) + f(n) & \text{if } n > 1 \end{cases}$$

where $a \geq 1$, $b > 1$ and $f(n)$ is a given function, we have the recurrence for the worst case running time of a divide and conquer algorithm that creates subproblems, each being of size $1/b$ of the original problem, and in which the combine steps together take $f(n)$ time.

When it comes to divide and conquer algorithms, it is often easier to come up with this recursion, but harder to derive the runtime complexity. Fortunately, there are at least three methods to provide "O" bounds for these recurrences: the substitution method, the recursion tree method, and the master method. For the purpose of this course, we will only focus on the master method.

Lesson 4.2.2 The Master Method

The master method provides a way to solve recurrences of the following form:

$T(n) = aT(n/b) + f(n)$

where

$a \geq 1$ and $b > 1$ are constants,

$f(n)$ is an asymptotically positive function

The master method consists of three cases, which will allow you to solve these kind of recurrences quite easily. Before we delve into these three cases, it is important to note that the recurrence is not actually well defined, since n/b may not be an integer. Whether we replace it with the floor or ceiling of the n/b division will not affect the asymptotic behavior of the recurrence.

The big O notation describes the asymptotic upper bound of the growth rate of a function. There are also other notations to describe bounds on the growth rate of functions.

For the purpose of the master method, we're interested in the big-theta notation (θ) and the big-omega notation (Ω).

The big-theta notation describes the asymptotic tight bound of the growth rate. It's called tight bound because the running time is nailed within a constant factor above and below. It is a tighter bound than $O(n)$.

When we say that an algorithm is $O(f(n))$, we're saying that the running time of the algorithm as n gets larger is at most proportional to $f(n)$.

When we say that an algorithm is $\theta(f(n))$, we're saying that the running time of the algorithm as n gets larger is proportional to $f(n)$.

The big-omega notation describes an asymptotic lower bound of the growth rate. When we say that an algorithm is $\Omega(f(n))$, we're saying that the running time of the algorithm as n gets larger is at least proportional to $f(n)$.

Having clarified all the necessary notations, we can present the three cases to derive the asymptotic bounds from a recurrence of type $T(n) = aT(n/b) + f(n)$ as follows:

1. If $f(n) = O(n^{\log_b a - \epsilon})$ for some constant $\epsilon > 0$, then

$$T(n) = \theta(n^{\log_b a}) = O(n^{\log_b a})$$

2. If $f(n) = \theta(n^{\log_b a})$, then
$$T(n) = \theta(n^{\log_b a} \log(n)) = O(n^{\log_b a} \log(n))$$

3. If $f(n) = \Omega(n^{\log_b a + \epsilon})$ for some constant $\epsilon > 0$, and

If a $f(n/b) \leq c\, f(n)$ for some constant $c < 1$ and all sufficiently large n, then
$$T(n) = T(n) = \theta(f(n)) = O(f(n))$$

Note that in all three cases we're comparing the function $f(n)$ with the function $n^{\log_b a}$. This function is usually called the "critical exponent."

We can see intuitively that the larger of the two functions determines the solution to the recurrence.

In Case 2, the functions are of the same size, so we multiply by a logarithmic factor.

One other way to see this is that in Case 1, the work to split and recombine a problem is dwarfed by subproblems; in Case 2, the work to split and recombine a problem is comparable to subproblems; and in Case 3, the work to split and recombine a problem dominates the subproblems.

To get some practice on using the master method, let's look at some examples.

For the first case, let's consider the following:

$$T(n) = 9T(n/3) + n$$

For this recurrence, we have $a = 9$, $b = 3$, $f(n) = n$, and thus we have $n^{\log_b a} = n^{\log_3 9} = \theta(n^2)$. Since $f(n) = \Omega(n^{\log_4 3 + \epsilon})$, ϵ being one, we can apply Case 1 of the master theorem and conclude that $T(n) = O(n2)$.

For the second case, let's consider the following:

$$T(n) = 2T(n/2) + 10(n)$$

For this recurrence, we have $a = 2, b = 2, f(n) = 10n$, and thus we have $n^{\log_b a} = n^{\log_2 2} = O(n)$. Since $f(n) = O(n)$, we can apply Case 2 of the master theorem and conclude that $T(n) = O(n\log n)$.

For the third and final case, let's consider the following:

$$T(n) = 3T(n/4) + n\log(n)$$

For this recurrence, we have $a = 3, b = 4, f(n) = n\log(n)$, and thus we have $n^{\log_b a} = n^{\log_4 3} = O(n^{0.793})$. Since $f(n) = \Omega(n^{\log_4 3 + \epsilon})$, being around 0.2, we can apply Case 3 as long as the condition holds for $f(n)$.

For sufficiently large n, we have $af(n/b) = 3(n/4) \log(n/4) <= (3/4) n\log n (for\ c = 3/4)$. Consequently, $T(n) = O(n\log n)$.

Lesson 4.2.3 The Closest Pair of Points Problem

Now that we know what characterizes a divide and conquer algorithm and are familiar with the master method to derive bounds from recurrences, let's look at a problem solvable by a divide and conquer approach.

The problem we will be looking at is the problem of finding the closest pair of points on a plane. We are given an array of n points in the plane, and we want to find out the closest pair of points in this array. Recall that the distance between two points, p and q, is given by the following:

$$\|pq\| = \sqrt{(p_x - q_x)^2 + (p_y - q_y)^2}$$

Our first approach may be to compute the distance between each pair and return the smallest, for a runtime complexity of $O(n^2)$. The code given in **Snippet 4.3** implements this algorithm.

Snippet 4.3   Brute force for closest pair of points. Source class name: `ClosestPairOfPoints`

```java
PointPair bruteForce(List<Point> points) {
    PointPair best = new PointPair(points.get(0), points.get(1));
    for (int i = 2; i < points.size(); i++) {
        for (int j = i - 1; j >= 0; j--) {
            PointPair candidate =
                new PointPair(points.get(i), points.get(j));
            if (candidate.distance() < best.distance())
                best = candidate;
        }
    }
    return best;
}
```

The proposed algorithm solves this problem, but we can do better by using a divide and conquer approach. The algorithm makes use of a preprocessing step in which it sorts the input array by its x coordinate. Then, it proceeds as follows:

1. **Divides** the array into two halves.
2. Recursively finds the smallest distances in both subarrays (**conquer**).
3. **Combines** the results by taking the minimum distance from both halves and additionally considers pairs so that one point in the pair is from the left subarray and another is from the right subarray.

The approach seems straightforward, except for the combine part. After finding the minimum distance d from both the left and right subarrays, we have an upper bound of the minimum distance for this subproblem. Therefore, we only need to consider points whose x coordinate is closer than d to the middle vertical line. We can then sort those points by y coordinates and find the smallest distance in the strip, as shown in **Figure 4.2**.

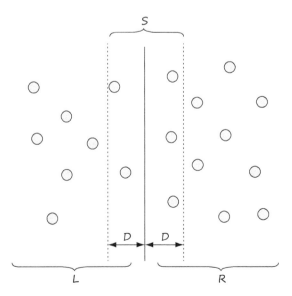

Figure 4.2   Method to calculate closest pair of points

The code in **Snippet 4.4** computes the minimum distance in the strip, considering the minimum distance computed so far.

Snippet 4.4   Computing the minimum distance between pairs of points in the middle strip. Source class name: `ClosestPairOfPoints`

```
        Collections.sort(sortedPoints, (o1, o2) -> Integer.
signum(o1.y - o2.y));
        for (int i = 0; i < points.size(); i++) {
            for (int j = i + 1; j < points.size() &&
                    (points.get(j).y - points.get(i).y) < best.
distance(); j++) {
                PointPair candidate = new PointPair(points.get(i),
points.get(j));
                if (candidate.distance() < best.distance())
                    best = candidate;
            }
        }
```

Looking at this code, it seems to have a runtime of $O(n^2)$, which doesn't really improve our brute force approach. However, it can be proved geometrically that for every point in the strip, a maximum of seven points after it need to be checked. This reduces the runtime of this step to $O(nlogn)$ due to the sorting step.

We can even do better on this step if we sort the initial input by the y-coordinate and keep a relationship between the points on the x-sorted array and the y-sorted array, effectively reducing the runtime of this step to $O(n)$.

After having computed the minimum distance from both subarrays and the middle strip, we have found the closest pair of points in the subarray. The following code snippet exposes the merging part of both subarrays and calling the `bestWithStrip()` method given in **Snippet 4.5**.

Snippet 4.5   Combine step of the divide and conquer algorithm to find the closest pair of points on a plane. Source class name: `ClosestPairOfPoints`

```
PointPair bestSoFar = bl;
if (br.distance() < bl.distance())
    bestSoFar = br;
        List<Point> strip = new ArrayList<>();
        for (int i = 0; i < N; i++) {
            if (Math.abs(points.get(i).x - midPoint.x) <
bestSoFar.distance())
                strip.add(points.get(i));
        }
        return bestWithStrip(strip, bestSoFar);
```

The proposed algorithm divides all points into two sets and recursively solves both subproblems. After dividing, it finds the strip in $O(n)$ time and finds the closest points in $O(n)$ time (we're assuming the improvement of not requiring the sort in this step). Therefore, $T(n)$ can be expressed as $T(n) = 2T(n/2) + O(n) + O(n) = 2T(n/2) + O(n)$, which is a bound of $O(nlogn)$, being better than the brute force approach.

Test yourself on this concept by completing Lab Activity 4.2: Solving the Maximum Subarray Problem.

There exists an even faster dynamic programming algorithm with a runtime of $O(n)$ to solve the maximum subarray problem. The algorithm is called Kadane's algorithm. Dynamic programming will be explored in the next lesson.

We introduced the divide and conquer paradigm of algorithm design. We formalized the steps that a divide and conquer algorithm goes through, and showed the students how to go from a recurrence relationship to a runtime complexity bound using the master theorem. To gain intuition about the applicability of divide and conquer algorithms, we explored the problem of finding the closest pair of points on a plane.

LESSON 4.3 UNDERSTANDING DYNAMIC PROGRAMMING

After greedy and divide and conquer, we will turn our attention to dynamic programming. Dynamic programming is an algorithm design paradigm that also attempts to solve optimization problems by combining solutions with subproblems. Unlike divide and conquer, subproblems need to exhibit optimal substructure for dynamic programming to be applicable.

Lesson 4.3.1 Elements of a Dynamic Programming Problem

There are two key ingredients that an optimization problem must have for dynamic programming to be applicable: optimal substructure and overlapping subproblems.

OPTIMAL SUBSTRUCTURE

Optimal substructure is something we already covered when we introduced greedy algorithms. Recall that a problem exhibits optimal substructure, if an optimal solution to the problem contains within it, the optimal solutions to the sub-problems. There's a common pattern when trying to discover optimal substructure for a problem that can be explained as follows:

- Show that a solution to the problem consists of making a choice, which leaves one or more subproblems to be solved. This choice may not be obvious and it is likely that many choices have to be tried (contrary to a greedy approach, in which a single optimal choice is made)
- Supposing that you are given the choice that leads to an optimal solution, determine the subproblems that follow
- Show that the solutions to the subproblems used within an optimal solution to the problem must themselves be optimal
- Usually, a "cut-and-paste" technique is used here. By supposing that each subproblem solution is not optimal, if a non-optimal solution is "cut out" and an optimal one is "pasted in," a better solution to the original problem is produced, contradicting the supposition that the original solution to the problem was optimal

OVERLAPPING SUBPROBLEMS

Another ingredient that optimization problems must have for dynamic programming to apply is that the space of subproblems should be "small." Hence, a recursive algorithm for the problem should solve the same subproblems repeatedly. Typically, the total number of distinct subproblems is a polynomial in the input size. A recursive algorithm is said to have overlapping subproblems if it visits the same problem repeatedly. It's therefore typical for dynamic programming algorithms to cache solutions to subproblems to avoid re-computation of the same solutions over and over.

Lesson 4.3.2 0-1 Knapsack

To showcase a dynamic programming solution, exploring the properties of the problem that make it solvable by this technique, we shall look at the "0-1 knapsack" problem.

You are given weights and values of n items. You must put these items in a knapsack of capacity W to get the maximum value of the knapsack. You cannot break an item. You can either pick it or not pick it (hence, the 0-1 property).

In other words, you are given two arrays, $values[0 \ldots n - 1]$ and $weights[0 \ldots n - 1]$, which represent values and weights associated with n items, respectively. You want to find the maximum value subset of $values[]$ such that the sum of weights of the subset is smaller than or equal to W.

The first immediate solution to this problem is to consider all subsets of items and calculate the total weight and value of all subsets, considering only those whose total weight is smaller than W. To consider all subsets of items, we can observe that there are two choices for each item: either it is included in the optimal subset, or it is not. Hence, the maximum value we can obtain from n items is the maximum of two values:

1. The maximum value obtained by $n - 1$ items and W weight (i.e., they don't include the nth item in the optimal solution).
2. The value of the nth item plus the maximum value obtained by $n - 1$ items and W minus the weight of the nth item (e.g., including the nth item).

With the previous observation, we've shown the optimal substructure property for the 0-1 knapsack problem.

> Practice this concept by completing Practice Exercise 4.3: Solving the 0-1 Knapsack Problem Using Recursion.

Figure 4.3 shows the diagram of tree for the recursion for n and W, with inputs $values[] = \{10,20,30\}$ and $weights[] = \{1,1,1\}$.

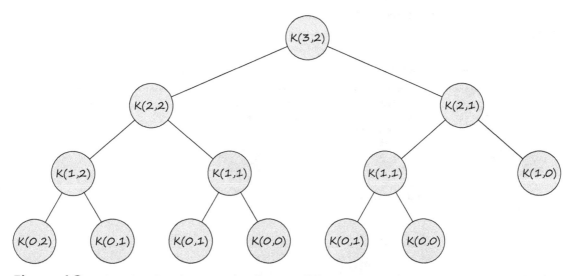

Figure 4.3   Tree showing the recursion for n and W

Since problems are evaluated again, this has the overlapping subproblems property. When we have a recursive top-down approach to a problem with the overlapping subproblems property, we can improve things by modifying the procedure to save the result of each subproblem (in an array or hash table). The procedure now first checks to see whether it has previously solved the subproblem. If so, it returns the saved value; if not, it computes, stores, and returns it. It is said that the recursive procedure has been memoized, remembering what results it has computed previously. Such an approach is therefore usually called top-down with memoization. **Snippet 4.7** adapts **Snippet 4.6** to use memoization.

Snippet 4.7   Top down with memoization approach for the 0-1 Knapsack problem. Source class name: `Knapsack`

```java
public int topDownWithMemoizationAux(int W, int weights[], int
    values[], int n, int[][] memo) {
    if (n == 0 || W == 0)
        return 0;
    if (memo[n][W] == -1) {
        if (weights[n - 1] > W)
            memo[n][W] = topDownWithMemoizationAux(W,
            weights,values, n - 1, memo);
        else
            memo[n][W] = Math.max(
            values[n - 1] + topDownWithMemoizationAux(W -
            weights[n - 1], weights, values, n - 1, memo),
            topDownWithMemoizationAux(W, weights, values, n -
                    1, memo));
        }
        return memo[n][W];
    }
```

By applying memoization, we reduce the runtime complexity of the algorithm from exponential (2^n) to quadratic ($n*W$). It is also possible to solve this problem using a bottom-up approach.

Use of a bottom-up approach typically depends on some natural notion of the "size" of the subproblems. We must sort the subproblems by size and solve them in order, smallest first, so that we're sure that we already have computed the solutions for smaller subproblems when we need them for a larger one.

A bottom-up approach usually yields the same asymptotic running time as a topdown approach, but it is typical for it to have much better constant factors, since it has less overhead for procedure calls. A bottom-up approach for solving the 0-1 Knapsack problem is shown in **Snippet 4.8**.

Snippet 4.8   Bottom-up approach for the 0-1 Knapsack problem. Source class name: `Knapsack`

```java
public int bottomUp(int weight, int weights[], int values[]) {
    int[][] dp = new int[values.length + 1][weight + 1];
    for (int i = 0; i <= values.length; i++) {
        for (int w = 0; w <= weight; w++) {
            if (i == 0 || w == 0)
                dp[i][w] = 0;
            else if (weights[i - 1] <= w)
                dp[i][w] = Math.max(values[i - 1] + dp[i - 1][w - weights[i
- 1]], dp[i - 1][w]);
            else
                dp[i][w] = dp[i - 1][w];
        }
    }
    return dp[values.length][weight];
}
```

Lesson 4.3.3 Longest Common Subsequence

Now, let's look at a different problem which is solvable by a dynamic programming algorithm. The problem we're now interested in is the longest common subsequence problem.

We're interested in finding similarities between two given sequences by computing the Longest **Common Subsequence (LCS)** between them. A common subsequence, S_3, of two given sequences, S_1 and S_2, is a sequence whose elements appear in both S_1 and S_2 in the same order, but not necessarily consecutively. This problem is usually applicable when finding DNA similarities of different organisms.

For example, if we have two strands, S_1 and S_2, as follows:

$S_1 = ACCGGTCGAGTGCGCGGAGCCGGCCGAA$
$S_2 = GTCGTTCGGAATGCCGTTGCTCTGTAAAA,$

Then the longest common strand between those two, let's call it S_3, would be as follows (see **Figure 4.4**):

$S_3 = GTCGTCGGAAGCCGGCCGAA.$

Figure 4.4   Calculating the longest common subsequence

This problem is solvable using dynamic programming. If we go for a brute force approach, we can enumerate all subsequences of S_1 and check each subsequence to see if it is also a subsequence of S_2, keeping track of the longest one we find.

However, if $|S_1| = m$, then S_1 has $2m$ ubsequences, making it impractical for long sequences. The **LCS** exhibits the optimal-substructure property.

One way for this to become evident is to think in terms of prefixes. Let's assume that we have the following two sequences:

$X = \{x_1, x_2 \ldots x_m\}$
$Y = \{y_1, y_2 \ldots y_n\}$

Let Z be any LCS of X and Y that can be represented as follows:

$Z = \{x_1, z_2 \ldots z_k\}$

Then, the following cases are possible:

2. If $x_m = y_n$, then $z_k = x_m = y_n$, and therefore $Z_k - 1$ is a LCS of $X_m - 1$ and $Y_n - 1$.
3. If $x_m ! = y_n$, then $z_k ! = x_m$ implies that Z is a LCS of $X_m - 1$ and Y.
4. If $x_m ! = y_n$ then $z_k ! = y_n$ implies that Z is a LCS of X and $Yn - 1$.

This tells us that an LCS of two sequences contains the LCS of prefixes of the two sequences, exhibiting the optimal-substructure property. If we define $c[i][j]$ to be the length of a LCS of sequences X_i and Y_j, then we can arrive at the following recursive formula, which guides us toward the dynamic programming solution for the problem that can be represented as follows:

$$c[i][j] = \begin{cases} 0 & \text{if } i = 0 \text{ or } j = 0, \\ c[i-1][j-1] + 1 & \text{if } i, j > 0 \text{ and } x_i = y_j, \\ max(c[i][j-1], c[i-1][j]) & \text{if } i, j > 0 \text{ and } x_i \neq y_j. \end{cases}$$

Looking at the recurrence, the property of overlapping subproblems immediately pops out.

To find a LCS of X and Y, we may need to find the LCS's of X and Y_{n-1} and X_{m-1} and Y, but each of these have the problem of finding the LCS of X_{m-1} and Y_{n-1}. Many other subproblems share sub-subproblems.

Using this recurrence, in a bottom-up fashion (where we have solutions for subproblems readily computed), we can produce the following dynamic programming algorithm to compute the length of the longest common subsequence of two strings as shown in **Snippet 4.9**.

Snippet 4.9:   Computing the length of the longest common subsequence of two strings using dynamic programming algorithm. Source class name: `LongestCommonSubsequence`

```java
public int length(String x, String y) {
    int m = x.length();
    int n = y.length();
    int[][] c = new int[m + 1][n + 1];
    for (int i = 1; i <= m; i++) {
        for (int j = 1; j <= n; j++) {
            if (x.charAt(i - 1) == y.charAt(j - 1))
                c[i][j] = c[i - 1][j - 1] + 1;
            else
                c[i][j] = Math.max(c[i - 1][j], c[i][j - 1]);} }
    return c[m][n];
}
```

It is possible to also compute the longest common subsequence, and not only the length of it if we keep track of the "direction" we go in the c matrix on each step (either up or left), taking into account that we only add a new character to the optimal subsequence when $x_i = y_i$.

Test yourself on this concept by completing Lab Activity 4.3: The Coin Change Problem.

In this lesson, we introduced the dynamic programming paradigm of algorithm design, using the 0-1 knapsack and the longest common subsequence problems as examples. We introduced the two properties a problem must observe to be optimally solved by a dynamic programming algorithm: optimal substructure and overlapping subproblems, and showed the students how to identify these properties. We've also seen the differences between a top-down (with memoization) and a bottom-up approach in dynamic programming algorithms.

SUMMARY

In this module, we have discussed three different algorithm design paradigms. We've seen example problems for all of them and discussed how we can identify whether problems may be solvable by one of the given paradigms. In the next module, we will be focusing on some string matching algorithms that use the paradigms introduced here.

STRING MATCHING ALGORITHMS

MODULE OBJECTIVES

BY THE END OF THIS MODULE, YOU WILL BE ABLE TO:

1. List common string matching algorithms
2. Solve the string matching problem
3. Devise a naive algorithm to solve the string matching problem
4. Implement the Boyer-Moore string search algorithm to carry out string search in literature

INTRODUCTION

String matching algorithms are quite common in text-editing programs. These kind of programs frequently need to find all occurrences of a pattern in the text, where the text is usually the document being edited and the pattern is a word supplied by the user. Since text-editing programs aim to be responsive, having efficient algorithms to solve the string matching problem is fundamental.

LESSON 5.1 NAIVE SEARCH ALGORITHM

The string matching problem has two inputs, as follows:

- An array $T[1, 2, ...n]$ of length n
- An array $P[1, 2, ...m]$ of length m $(<= n)$

The elements of T and P are characters from the same finite alphabet (usually called Σ).

For instance, we may be searching in binary strings, in which case our alphabet is {0, 1}, or we may be searching in strings of lowercase letters, in which case our alphabet is {a, b … z}.

The following diagram represents this terminology:

Figure 5.1   Representation of text array *T*, pattern array *P*, and finite alphabet *Σ*

The character arrays P and T are usually called "strings of characters." We're interested in finding occurrences of pattern *P* in text *T*.

We say that pattern *P* occurs in text *T* if we can align the pattern *P* with text *T* so that all characters in *P* match the ones in *T*. When aligning, we need to shift pattern *P* zero or more times to the right.

Therefore, in the string matching problem, we're interested in valid shifts with which pattern *P* occurs in text *T*. We say that the pattern *P* occurs with a shift *s* in text *T* if the pattern *P* occurs beginning at position *s* + 1 in text *T*. In other words, we need to shift *P* from the start of text *T* *s* times to the right, in order to find a match. In its essence, the string matching problem aims to find all valid shifts with which pattern *P* occurs in a given text *T*.

Two common examples, besides text-editing programs, are finding patterns in DNA sequences and finding web pages that are relevant to queries in internet search engines.

Now that we've formalized the string matching problem, let's look at the naive algorithm to solve it.

Lesson 5.1.1 Implementing Naive Search

As we described the string matching problem, we said that we were interested in finding all valid shifts with which pattern *P* occurs in a given text *T*. If we translate that notion directly into an algorithm, we're able to arrive at the naive string matching algorithm.

> Practice this concept by completing Practice Exercise 5.1: Developing the String Matching Algorithm in Java.

 NOTE   The implementation of the naive string matching algorithm is an almost direct translation of the problem statement. We want to go through all possible shifts for *P* and check which ones are valid by comparing each element of *P* with the corresponding shifted elements of *T*.

A possible solution for this problem is in **Snippet 5.1**.

Snippet 5.1   Solution to the Naive String Matching Problem. Source class name: `solution.`
`NaiveStringMatching`

```
for (int i = 0; i < n - m + 1; i++) {
    boolean hasMatch = true;
    for (int j = 0; j < m; j++) {
        if (P.charAt(j) != T.charAt(i + j)) {
            hasMatch = false;
            break;
        }
    }
    if (hasMatch)
        shifts.add(i);
}
```

Lesson 5.1.2 Rationalization of the Naive Search Algorithm

The naive search algorithm takes $O((n - m + 1)m)$ time, which is a tight bound on the worst case. We can imagine a worst case of the naive search algorithm if we have a text string with the character a repeating for n times, that is, an (such as $a5 = $ "$aaaaa$"), and the pattern am (for $m <= n$). In this case, we have to execute the inner loop `m` times to validate the shift.

The naive search algorithm can be improved if we know that all characters in pattern P are different. In this case, whenever we fail validating a shift because `P[j]` doesn't match `T[i + j]`, we don't need to backtrack. Instead, we can start validating the next shift on `(i + j)`, therefore reducing the running time of the algorithm to $O(n)$.

For example, if `P = "abcd"` and `T = "abcaabcd"`, when `i = 0` and `j = 3`, we find a mismatch (`'a'! = 'd'`). Instead of repeating the comparisons for `i = 1`, we can start on `i = 3`, because we're sure there's no other a between `i = 0` and `i = 3` (remember that all characters of P are different). These kinds of observations on the pattern P are the basis of the Boyer-Moore algorithm.

In this lesson, we introduced the string matching problem and solved it using a naive algorithm. In the following lesson, we'll introduce a much more efficient algorithm to solve this problem – the Boyer-Moore algorithm.

LESSON 5.2 GETTING STARTED WITH THE BOYER-MOORE STRING SEARCHING ALGORITHM

The Boyer-Moore string searching algorithm was introduced by Robert S. Boyer and J. Strother Moore in 1977, and builds upon the naive search algorithm by intelligently skipping certain sections of the text.

One key feature of the algorithm is that it matches the pattern from right to left, instead of left to right, using to its advantage a couple of shift rules that improve its running time. To understand the effect of these rules, let's build the Boyer-Moore algorithm from our naive search algorithm.

We'll start by modifying the matching on the pattern so that it operates from right to left. The code shown in **Snippet 5.2** demonstrates this.

Snippet 5.2   Modifying the inner loop from Snippet 5.1 for algorithm to operate from right to left

```java
for (int j = m - 1; j >= 0; j--) {
    if (P.charAt(j) != T.charAt(i + j)) {
        hasMatch = false;
        break;
    }
}
```

Using the naive string matching algorithm as the base, let's look at some rules that allow us to intelligently skip certain shifts.

Lesson 5.2.1 The Bad Character Rule

The idea of the bad character rule is to identify mismatches between a character in the pattern and a character in the text so that we can safely skip certain shifts. To identify the occurrence of a bad character, let's look at the example in **Table 5.1**.

Table 5.1   Identifying bad characters

i	0	1	2	3	4	5	6	7	8	9	10	11	12	13	14	15	16
T	H	C	B	B	A	H	C	C	A	B	A	H	A	H	B	C	C
P	A	B	A	H	A	H											

In the example provided in **Table 5.1**, we successfully matched the suffix *AH*, but then arrived at a bad character, since $B! = H$. Whenever this happens, we're sure that it will only be possible to find a valid shift starting from the next shift that solves this mismatch. This means that we can shift *P* until either of the following conditions are true:

1. The mismatch is turned into a match.

2. The pattern moves past the mismatched character.

We can turn a mismatch into a match whenever the pattern has characters to the left of the mismatched character that match the character in the text. Otherwise, we must move the pattern past the mismatched character. In the example provided in **Table 5.1**, we have another *B* at $P[1]$, so we can shift *P* until $P[1]$ aligns with $T[3]$ as shown in **Table 5.2**.

Table 5.2   Using the bad character rule to skip a shift

i	0	1	2	3	4	5	6	7	8	9	10	11	12	13	14	15	16
T	H	C	B	B	A	H	C	C	A	B	A	H	A	H	B	C	C
P			A	B	A	H	A	H									

We've safely skipped the check for 1 shift. Now, we have a mismatch right in the first character. Let's try to apply the bad character rule. First, let's see if we can turn the mismatch into a match. Unfortunately, that is not possible because the character *C* is absent from *P*. In this case, we shift the pattern past the mismatched character as shown in **Table 5.3**.

Table 5.3   Pattern moving past a mismatched character

i	0	1	2	3	4	5	6	7	8	9	10	11	12	13	14	15	16
T	H	C	B	B	A	H	C	C	A	B	A	H	A	H	B	C	C
P									A	B	A	H	A	H			

We've successfully skipped checking five shifts and have arrived at a valid shift.

The bad character rule will help us optimize the naive string matching algorithm, but only if we can efficiently find the correct number of times to shift. Let's assume we have access to a two dimensional array [1...m] [1...e], e being the size of our alphabet. For convenience, let's call this array left and assume that left[i][j] gives us the closest index k of character j in P so that k < i, or is −1 if character j isn't found to the left of i in P. If we're able to build such an array, we could improve our naive string search algorithm by considering possibly larger skips (given by the information in left). **Snippet 5.3** shows how we can use the left array to improve our naive string searching algorithm.

Snippet 5.3   Using the bad character rule to improve our skips

```
int skip;
for (int i = 0; i < n - m + 1; i += skip) {
    skip = 0;
    for (int j = m - 1; j >= 0; j--) {
        if (P.charAt(j) != T.charAt(i + j)) {
            skip = Math.max(1, j - left[j][T.charAt(i + j)]);
            break;
        }
    }
    if (skip == 0) {
        shifts.add(i);
        skip = 1;
    }
}
```

We're left to filling in the left array, which will be performed in the next activity.

Test yourself on this concept by completing Lab Activity 5.2: Implementing the Bad Character Rule.

Lesson 5.2.2 The Good Suffix Rule

The good suffix rule presents a complementary method to enhance our search for valid shifts. To identify when the good suffix rule is applicable, let's look at the example given in **Table 5.4**.

Table 5.4   Illustration of the good suffix rule

i	0	1	2	3	4	5	6	7	8	9	10	11	12	13	14	15	16	17
T	A	A	B	A	B	A	B	A	C	B	A	C	A	B	B	C	A	B
P	A	A	C	C	A	C	C	A	C									

When found in a situation where we have matched a suffix of P but have found a mismatch, using the good suffix rule, and considering t as the matched suffix, we can try to find the next shift that solves the mismatch by carrying out either of the following cases:

1. Find another occurrence of t to the left in P.

2. Find a prefix of P which matches a suffix of t.

3. Move P past t.

Considering *Case 1*, we can try to shift P by three to align other occurrences of t in P (starting at P[4]). As we can see, the letter to the left of that occurrence of t (in P[3]) is C, which is exactly the same as the one that provoked the mismatch. Therefore, we should always try to find a t that is followed, on the left, by a character that is different from the one that provoked the mismatch. A variant of the good suffix rule which ignores the character on the left of t is called the weak good suffix rule.

 NOTE   The good suffix rule takes into account that the character on the left of t is also called the strong good suffix rule.

If we can't find another occurrence of t in P, the best we can do with this rule is to find a prefix of P that matches a suffix of t, entering *Case 2*. **Table 5.5** illustrates this case.

Table 5.5   Finding prefix of P matching the suffix of T

i	0	1	2	3	4	5	6	7	8	9	10
T	A	A	B	A	B	A	B	A	C	B	A
P	A	B	B	A	B						

In this case, we found a mismatch at P[1], but we can't find another occurrence of *BAB* to the left of it. We can, however, find a prefix of *AB* that matches a suffix of t *AB* and shift P so that these align.

Whenever we can neither find another occurrence nor a prefix of t, we're left with moving P past t in T.

The implementation of the good suffix rule also requires some preprocessing on P. To understand the preprocessing that is necessary, we need to introduce the concept of a border and proper prefix and suffix. A prefix of string S is a substring of S that occurs at the beginning of S. A proper prefix of string S is a prefix of S that is different than S (consider that S is always a prefix of S). A suffix of string S is a substring of S that occurs at the end of S. A proper suffix of string S is a suffix of S that is different from S (consider that S is always a suffix of S). A border is a substring of a given string that is both a proper prefix and a proper suffix. For example, given the string *ccacc*, there are two borders: *c* and *cc*. *cca* is not a border.

The preprocessing step for the good suffix rule is divided into two steps: one for *Case 1* of the rule, and another for *Case 2*.

In *Case 1*, the matching suffix is a border of a suffix of a pattern. For example, if P = *AACCACCAC* and we have t = *AC* (a suffix of P), then we need to find a suffix of P that has *AC* as a prefix (constituting a border of the suffix). The string *ACCAC* is a suffix of P and has *AC* as a border.

Therefore, we need to find the borders of the suffixes of the pattern. But, even after finding them, we need to be able to map a given border to the shortest suffix that has this border so that we're able to shift accordingly. Moreover, to follow the strong good suffix rule, the border cannot be extended to the left by the same symbol that caused the mismatch.

The preprocessing algorithm for *Case 1* is displayed in **Snippet 5.4**.

Snippet 5.4   Preprocessing algorithm for case 1 of the good suffix rule. Source class name: `GoodSuffixRule`

```
int i = m, j = m + 1;
int[] f = new int[m + 1];
int[] s = new int[m + 1];

f[i] = j;
while (i > 0) {
    while (j <= m && P.charAt(i - 1) != P.charAt(j - 1)) {
        if (s[j] == 0)
            s[j] = j - i;
        j = f[j];
    }
    i--; j--;
    f[i] = j;
}
```

> **NOTE**   To better understand the preprocessing algorithm for *Case 1*, put some `println` statements on the relevant steps of the algorithm and run it using some sample input. You can use string *ABBABAB*, whose output is shown in **Table 5.6**.

In **Snippet 5.4**, we compute an array `f`, whose entries `f[i]` contain the starting position of the widest border of the suffix of the pattern that starts at position i. `f[m]` is equal to $m+1$, as the empty string has no border. The idea behind the previously shown preprocessing algorithm is to compute each border by checking whether a shorter border that is already known can be extended to the left by the same symbol. The array `s` is used to store shift distances; we can save entries in array `s` whenever we can't extend a border to the left (when `P[i - 1] != P[j - 1]`), provided that `s[j]` is not already occupied.

To better understand what this algorithm produces, let's look at its output for string *ABBABAB*, which is shown **Table 5.6**.

Table 5.6   Output of the preprocessing algorithm for case 1 of the good suffix rule with string *ABBABAB*

i	0	1	2	3	4	5	6	7
P	A	B	B	A	B	A	B	
f	5	6	4	5	6	7	7	8
s	0	0	0	0	2	0	4	1

The widest border of suffix *BABAB*, which starts at 2, is *BAB*, which starts at 4, and therefore $f[2] = 4$. The widest border of suffix *AB*, which starts at 5, is "", which starts at 7. Therefore, $f[5] = 7$. The suffix *BABAB*, whose widest border is *BAB*, cannot be extended to the left (since $P[1]! = P[3]$). Therefore, the shift distance of *BAB* is matched and then a mismatch occurs, which is $s[4] = 4 - 2 = 2$. The suffix *BABAB* has border *B* as well, which also cannot be extended to left, which ensures that $s[6] = 6 - 2 = 4$. The suffix *B* beginning at position 6 has border "", beginning at position 7; therefore $s[7] = 7 - 6 = 1$, which corresponds to the shift distance if nothing has matched.

In *Case 2*, a suffix of the matching suffix of the pattern occurs at the beginning of the pattern, which constitutes a border of the pattern. Therefore, the pattern can be shifted as far as its widest border allows. What we need to do for the preprocessing step for *Case 2* is to find, for each suffix, the widest border of the pattern that is contained in that suffix. We can build upon the f array that was previously computed to do that. **Snippet 5.5** illustrates this.

Snippet 5.5   Preprocessing algorithm for case 2 of the good suffix rule. Source class name: `GoodSuffixRule`

```
j = f[0];
for (i = 0; i <= m; i++) {
    if (s[i] == 0)
        s[i] = j;
    if (i == j)
        j = f[j];
}
```

The widest border of the pattern is stored at $f[0]$. The idea of the preprocessing algorithm for *Case 2* is to use that value until the pattern becomes shorter than $f[0]$, in which case we go with the next wider border of the pattern ($f[j]$).

Integrating the good suffix case with the naive search algorithm allows us to improve on the skips performed, as shown in **Snippet 5.6**.

Snippet 5.6   The Boyer-Moore algorithm using only the good suffix rule. Source class name: `Goodsuffixrule`

```
for (i = 0; i < n - m + 1; i += skip) {
        boolean hasMatch = true;
        skip = 0;
        for (j = m - 1; j >= 0; j--) {
            if (P.charAt(j) != T.charAt (i + j)) {
skip = s[j + 1];
                hasMatch = false;
                break;
            }
        }
        if (hasMatch) {
            shifts.add(i);
            skip = s[0];
        }   }
```

Lesson 5.2.3 Application of the Boyer-Moore Algorithm

The Boyer-Moore algorithm is typically used with one or both the bad character and good suffix rule. When used with both rules, the shift that is to occur is the biggest one produced by the rules. The Boyer-Moore algorithm improves the naive search algorithm in the average case, but is still $O(nm)$ in the worst case (that case being the same described in the previous lesson, that is, a repeated group of characters both in the pattern and in the text).

Practice this concept by completing Practice Exercise 5.2: Implementing the Boyer-Moore Algorithm.

In this lesson, we've introduced the Boyer-Moore algorithm as an improvement over the naive search algorithm. By preprocessing the pattern to skip unnecessary shifts, we can decrease the average runtime complexity of the string matching algorithm. In the following lesson, we will list some other string matching algorithms, listing their applicability, but without going into much detail about their implementation.

LESSON 5.3 INTRODUCING OTHER STRING MATCHING ALGORITHMS

Even though the Boyer-Moore string search algorithm is the standard benchmark for practical string search literature, there are other string matching algorithms that are also suitable for different purposes. In this lesson, we present the following three, which are the most famous ones:

- Rabin-Karp
- Knuth-Morris-Pratt
- Aho-Corasick

However, we will only give out the implementation of Rabin-Karp.

Lesson 5.3.1 Rabin-Karp

In 1987, Richard M. Karp and Michael O. Rabin proposed a string matching algorithm that performs well in practice and generalizes string matching against a set of patterns. The Rabin-Karp algorithm takes $O(m)$ time in its preprocessing stage and its worst-case running time is $O((n - m + 1)m)$, similar to Boyer-Moore's.

To better introduce the Rabin-Karp algorithm, let's assume that our alphabet Σ is composed only of decimal digits ($\Sigma = \{0, 1, 2, 3, 4, 5, 6, 7, 8, 9\}$) , so that we can view a string of k characters as a decimal number with length k. Therefore, string 12345 corresponds to number 12345. Given a pattern $P[0 \ldots m]$ and a substring from text $T[i \ldots i + m]$, if we convert both those strings to their correspondent decimal number, so that we have numbers p and t_i, then $p = t_i$ only if $P[0 \ldots m] = T[i \ldots i + m]$, and therefore i is only a valid shift if $p = t_i$.

If we could compute p in $O(m)$ time and all the t_i values in $O(n - m + 1)$ time, then we could determine all valid shifts in $O(n)$ time by comparing p with each of the t_i values. The problem with this is when p and t_i are too large to work with. If the numbers are too large, then we can work with them modulo q, for a suitable modulus q. Let's leave the choice of a suitable modulus q for later. How we can generalize this to work with other alphabets? For example, what if we want to use characters that are not decimal digits?

Consider that, in the case of our original alphabet, to convert a string 12345 into a number, we would perform the operation $10^4 * 1 + 10^3 * 2 + 10^2 * 3 + 10^1 * 4 + 10^0 * 5$. If we have a D-ary alphabet $\{0, 1 \ldots d - 1\}$, then we could use the same strategy, but replace 10 by d. One other consideration to have is that, when we have computed t_i and we want to compute t_{i+1}, then we can simply remove the leftmost digit, shift everything to the left, and add the newest digit, that is, $t_{i+1} = ((t_i - T[i]^* d_{m-1})^* d + T[i + 1]) \% q$.

One final consideration to have is that working with modulo q is not perfect. $t_i = p \ (mod \ q)$ does not imply that $t_i = p$. But if $t_i' = p \ (mod \ q)$, then $t_i! = p$. We can therefore use this as a fast heuristic test to rule out invalid shifts.

> Practice this concept by completing Practice Exercise 5.3: Applying the Rabin-Karp Algorithm.

In the previous implementation, we chose q as a large prime number (using the BigInteger API). We did that so that we have a good hash function and avoided the most of false positives from the $p = t_i$ comparison. This is a similar technique to the one we saw in the remainder method for hash tables in Module 3, Hash Tables and Binary Search Trees.

NOTE The Rabin-Karp algorithm generalizes well to having a set of patterns to be found in the same text. For that purpose, it is frequently used in plagiarism detection.

Lesson 5.3.2 Knuth-Morris-Pratt

The Knuth-Morris-Pratt (KMP) algorithm is a single-pattern string searching algorithm conceived by Donald Knuth and Vaughan Pratt in 1970, and independently by James H. Morris, being jointly published by the three in 1977. When compared to the Boyer-Moore algorithm, KMP employs the observation that, when a mismatch occurs, the pattern embodies sufficient information to determine where the next match could begin.

It is similar to Boyer-Moore in the sense that it efficiently skips unnecessary comparisons. The KMP algorithm has a running time of $O(n)$.

Lesson 5.3.3 Aho-Corasick

The Aho-Corasick algorithm is a string searching algorithm invented by Alfred V. Aho and Margaret J. Corasick. Similar to the extended version of the Rabin-Karp algorithm, it is capable of matching elements of a dictionary (set of words) within an input text. The idea behind it is to build a finite state machine that enables matching all strings of the dictionary simultaneously. The algorithm is linear in the length of the strings, plus the length of the searched text, plus the number of output matches. If n is the length of the searched text, m is the sum of the length of all words in the dictionary, and z is the total number of occurrences of words in the text. Therefore, the time complexity of the Aho-Corasick algorithm is $O(n + m + z)$.

In this lesson, we've looked at three other famous string matching algorithms. Without going into much detail about them, we've seen their applicability on different problems other than the one the Boyer-Moore algorithm solves. In particular, we've noted that there are algorithms specialized for the finding of a set of patterns in a text.

SUMMARY

In this module, we have introduced the string matching problem. We've started from the naive search algorithm and improved it by using the rules introduced by Boyer and Moore. We've seen how these rules improve the average runtime complexity of our algorithm. We've also explored some other string matching algorithms without going into too much detail about them. In the next module, we will be exploring graphs and their applications.

GRAPHS, PRIME NUMBERS, AND COMPLEXITY CLASSES

MODULE OBJECTIVES

BY THE END OF THIS MODULE, YOU WILL BE ABLE TO:

1. Explain the common problems associated with graphs
2. Write an algorithm to compute prime numbers up to a certain limit
3. List different applications of graphs
4. Identify different complexity classes of problems

INTRODUCTION

Graph problems are very common in computer science, and their applications pervade many real-life applications. Everything that can be represented by entities and their relationships can ultimately be modeled by a graph. How we connect with friends on social media, how route–planning applications are able to find the shortest route, and how e-commerce websites are able to provide us with recommendations are all examples of problems modelled by graphs.

A graph is a structure composed of a set of objects in which some pairs of objects are related. The objects are modelled by the mathematical abstraction of vertices (sometimes also called nodes), and the pairwise relationships are modelled by the mathematical abstraction of edges (sometimes also called arcs).

Edges can be directed or undirected. A directed edge is an edge which has a direction associated with it. A graph that is composed of directed edges is called a directed graph. A graph that is composed of undirected edges is called an undirected graph. In a directed edge, it is common to call the start of the edge the head and the end of the edge the tail. In a directed graph, the out-degree of a vertex is the number of edges whose head is adjacent to it. The in-degree of a vertex is the number of edges whose tail is adjacent to it.

Figure 6.1 gives an example of a directed graph with *six* nodes and *eight* edges.

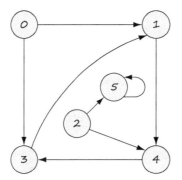

Figure 6.1   A directed graph

Figure 6.2 gives an example of an undirected graph with *five* nodes and *seven* edges.

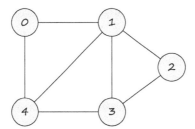

Figure 6.2   An undirected graph

Before we dive into how to represent a graph in a computer program, it is important to describe how the runtime of graph algorithms is usually characterized. As previously stated, a graph, G, can be seen as a set of vertices and edges, that is, $G = (V, E)$. As such, the size of the input is usually measured in terms of the number of vertices ($|V|$) and the number of edges ($|E|$). So, instead of relying solely on a single input size, N, the runtime of graph algorithms usually refers to both $|V|$ and $|E|$. In big O notation, it is common to use V to denote $|V|$ and E to denote $|E|$. For example, an algorithm that runs in time proportional to the number of vertices multiplied by the number of edges is said to run in time $O(VE)$.

LESSON 6.1 REPRESENTING GRAPHS

There are usually two standard ways to represent a graph $G = (V, E)$ in a computer program:

1. As a collection of adjacency lists.

2. As an adjacency matrix.

You can use either way to represent both directed and undirected graphs. We'll start by looking at the adjacency list representation.

Lesson 6.1.1 Adjacency List Representation

The adjacency list representation of a graph consists of an array of $|V|$ lists, one for each vertex in V. For each vertex u in V, there's a list containing all vertices v so that there is an edge connecting u and v in E. **Figure 6.3** shows the adjacency list representation of the directed graph in Figure 6.1.

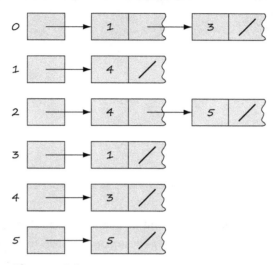

Figure 6.3   Adjacency list representation of the directed graph in Figure 6.1

For undirected graphs, we follow a similar strategy and build the adjacency list as if it were a directed graph with two edges between each pair of vertices u and v, which are (u, v) and (v, u). **Figure 6.4** shows the adjacency list representation of the undirected graph in Figure 6.2.

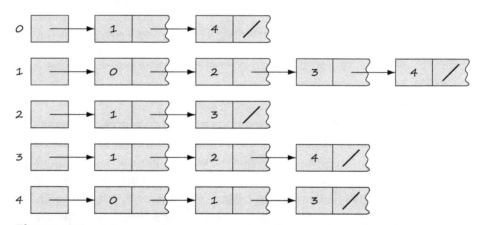

Figure 6.4   Adjacency list representation of the undirected graph in Figure 6.2

If G is a directed graph, the sum of the lengths of all the adjacency lists is $|E|$, as each edge constitutes a single node in one of the adjacency lists.

If G is an undirected graph, the sum of the lengths of all the adjacency lists is $2*|E|$, since each edge (u, v) appears twice, that is, once in u's and once in v's adjacency list.

For both types of graphs, the adjacency list representation has the property of requiring an amount of memory equal to $O(V + E)$.

Snippet 6.1 shows how to create a graph using the adjacency list representation in Java.

Snippet 6.1   Implementation of an adjacency list representation of a graph. Source class name:
`AdjacencyListGraph`

```java
public class AdjacencyListGraph {
    ArrayList<Integer>[] adj;
    public AdjacencyListGraph(int nodes) {
        this.adj = new ArrayList[nodes];
        for (int i = 0; i < nodes; i++)
            this.adj[i] = new ArrayList<>();
    }
    public void addEdge(int u, int v) {
        adj[u].add(v);
    }
}
```

It is common for one to have weighted graphs, that is, graphs in which each edge has an associated weight. The adjacency list representation is robust enough to support different graph variants, since we can store different edge representations in the adjacency lists.

 NOTE   We can store different edge representations in adjacency lists because we store the edges them-selves, thereby allowing customizable representations.

Practice this concept by completing Practice Exercise 6.1: Writing a Code to Add Weights to the Directed Graph.

Lesson 6.1.2 Adjacency Matrix Representation

The adjacency list representation of a graph provides a compact way to represent sparse graphs, for example, those for which $|E|$ is much less than $|V|^2$. Even though it is a representation that is useful for a lot of algorithms (which we will visit later), it does not support some features. For example, one cannot quickly tell whether there is an edge connecting two given vertices. In order to determine if u and v are connected, one has to go through the adjacency list of u to find an edge connecting it to v. Since the adjacency list of u can have at most E edges, this procedure runs in $O(E)$ time. One alternative representation that remedies this disadvantage at the cost of using asymptotically more memory is the adjacency matrix representation.

In this representation, a graph $G = (V, E)$ is represented by a $|V| \times |V|$ matrix $A = (a_{ij})$, where a_{ij} equals 1 if there's an edge (i, j) and 0 otherwise. **Table 6.1** shows the adjacency matrix representation of the directed graph of Figure 6.1.

Table 6.2 shows the adjacency matrix representation of the undirected graph of Figure 6.2.

The adjacency matrix representation of a graph requires $O(V^2)$ memory, independent of the number of edges in the graph. One thing to note on the adjacency matrix representation of undirected graphs is that the matrix is symmetrical along the main diagonal, since (u, v) and (v, u) represent the same edge. As such, the adjacency matrix of an undirected graph is its own transpose $(A = A^T)$. Taking advantage of this symmetry, one can cut on the memory needed to store the graph almost in half, as you don't need the array of each vertex to have size V. If i tracks the index of vertices in V, the size of array[i] can decrease by one as i increases by one.

Table 6.1   Adjacency matrix representation of the directed graph of Figure 6.1

	0	1	2	3	4	5
0	0	1	0	1	0	0
1	0	0	0	0	1	0
2	0	0	0	0	1	1
3	0	1	0	0	0	0
4	0	0	0	1	0	0
5	0	0	0	0	0	0

Table 6.2   Adjacency matrix representation of the undirected graph of Figure 6.2

	0	1	2	3	4
0	0	1	0	0	1
1	1	0	1	1	1
2	0	1	0	1	0
3	0	1	1	0	1
4	1	1	0	1	0

Snippet 6.3 shows how to create a graph using the adjacency matrix representation in Java:

Snippet 6.3   Implementation of an adjacency matrix representation of a directed graph. Source class name: `AdjacencyMatrixGraph`

```
public class AdjacencyMatrixGraph {
    int[][] adj;
    public AdjacencyMatrixGraph(int nodes) {
        this.adj = new int[nodes][nodes];
    }
    public void addEdge(int u, int v) {
        this.adj[u][v] = 1;
    }
}
```

The adjacency matrix representation is also robust enough to support different graph variants. In order to support weighted graphs, for example, one can store the weight of the edge in a_{ij}, instead of just one. The adjacency list representation is asymptotically at least as space-efficient as the adjacency matrix representation, but adjacency matrices are simpler, so they might be preferable when the graphs are reasonably small or dense. As previously stated, a sparse graph is one in which $|E|$ is much less than $|V|^2$, whereas a dense graph is one in which $|E|$ is closer to $|V|^2$. The adjacency list representation is more memory-efficient for sparse graphs. For dense graphs, an adjacency matrix representation is better suited, as it possibly takes less memory due to list pointers.

> Test yourself by completing Lab Activity 6.1: Building the Adjacency Matrix Representation of a Weighted Undirected Graph.

In this lesson, we learned two different ways of representing a graph in a computer program. We briefly examined the pros and cons of each representation, and we will take a look at their usefulness when implementing graph algorithms in the following lessons.

LESSON 6.2 TRAVERSING A GRAPH

A common activity on a graph is visiting each vertex of it in a given order. We will start by introducing the breadth-first search, and then follow with depth-first search. Both of these techniques form the archetype for many important graph algorithms, as we will see later with the cycle detection and Dijkstra's algorithm for single-source shortest paths.

Lesson 6.2.1 Breadth-First Search

Given a graph $G = (V, E)$ and a source vertex s, breadth-first search explores the edges of G systematically to discover every vertex that is reachable from s. While doing so, it computes the smallest number of edges from s to each reachable vertex, making it suitable to solve the single-source shortest path problem on unweighted graphs, or graphs whose edges all have the same weight.

Breadth-First Search (BFS) is named so because it expands the frontier between discovered and undiscovered vertices uniformly across the breadth of the frontier. In that sense, the algorithm first explores vertices at distance k from s before discovering vertices at distance $k + 1$. To keep track of progress, breadth-first search identifies each vertex as undiscovered, discovered, or expanded. All vertices start out undiscovered. A vertex is discovered the first time it is encountered during search, and is expanded when all the vertices adjacent to it have been discovered.

BFS constructs a breadth-first tree, rooted at source vertex s. Whenever the search discovers an undiscovered vertex v when scanning the outward edges of already discovered vertex u, the vertex v and the edge (u, v) are added to the tree. Therefore, u becomes the parent of v in the breadth-first tree. Since a vertex is discovered at most once, it has at most one parent. In order to illustrate this, let's look at a run of breadth-first searches for the directed graph of Figure 6.1 , starting at node 2, in **Table 6.3**.

Table 6.3   A run of BFS on the directed graph of Figure 6.1, Starting at Node 2

Step	Current Node	Discovered	Expanded	Undiscovered	Tree
0	2	{2}	{}	{0, 1, 3, 4, 5}	
1	4	{2, 4, 5}	{2}	{0, 1, 3}	
2	5	{2, 4, 5, 3}	{2, 4}	{0, 1}	

Step	Current Node	Discovered	Expanded	Undiscovered	Tree
3	3	{2, 4, 5, 3, 1}	{2, 4, 5}	{0}	
4	1	{2, 4, 5, 3, 1}	{2, 4, 5, 3}	{0}	
5	-	{2, 4, 5, 3, 1}	{2, 4, 5, 3, 1}	{0}	

There are a lot of insights to take from the breadth-first tree. For instance, the path from the root to a given node in the tree is the shortest path (in terms of edges) from those two vertices. Another thing to note is that vertices that are not in the breadth-first tree (as is the case of 0) are unreachable from the root vertex.

We previously saw how to perform the breadth-first search on trees. BFS on graphs is similar, but we need to keep track of explored nodes so that we don't get stuck in cycles. In order to implement breadth-first search, we will assume that our graph is represented using adjacency lists. We will attach certain attributes to each vertex in the graph that will allow us to guide our search and later construct the breadth-first tree. We will also use a first-in, first-out queue (covered in *Module 2, Sorting Algorithms and Fundamental Data Structures*) to manage the set of discovered vertices. **Snippet 6.4** illustrates the implementation of breadth-first search.

Snippet 6.4   Implementation of breadth-first search. Source class name: `BFS.Graph`

```java
Queue<Integer> q = new LinkedList<>();
q.add(start);
while (!q.isEmpty()) {
    int current = q.remove();
    for (int i = 0; i < this.adj[current].size(); i++) {
        int next = this.adj[current].get(i);
        if (!visited[next]) {
            visited[next] = true;
            parent[next] = current;
            q.add(next);
        }
    }
}
```

Let's focus on the implementation of the BFS function. We will start by initializing a couple of auxiliary arrays: `parent` and `visited`. The first one will hold, at `parent[i]`, the parent of node *i* in the breadth-first tree. The second one will tell us, at `visited[i]`, whether or not vertex i has been discovered. We start by discovering the starting node and adding it to a queue. The queue will keep those vertices that have been discovered but not yet expanded. As such, while there are still elements in the queue, we will take its first element, go through its adjacent vertices, and discover those that haven't already been discovered, adding them to the queue.

When the queue becomes empty, we're sure of having expanded all vertices that are reachable from the starting vertex.

In the previous implementation, we've returned the array of parent nodes of the breadth-first tree in the `bfs()` function, allowing us to reconstruct the paths. If not necessary, you could just return the size of paths, or any other information we might be interested in extracting from the breadth-first search traversal.

In the `bfs()` method, we're sure of enqueuing, and hence dequeuing, each vertex at most once. As such, the total time dedicated to queue operations is $O(V)$. After dequeuing each vertex, we scan its adjacency list. Since we dequeue each vertex at most once, we scan each adjacency list at most once. As the sum of lengths of all the adjacency lists is $O(E)$, the total time spent in scanning adjacency lists is $O(E)$. Therefore, the BFS procedure has an initialization time of $O(V)$ and a total running time of $O(V + E)$, running in linear time to the size of the adjacency list representation of *G*.

As we will see in later lessons, the BFS procedure is the archetype for many important graph algorithms.

Lesson 6.2.2 Depth-First Search

Given a graph $G = (V, E)$ and a source vertex *s,* depth-first search explores the edges of the graph by going "deeper" in the graph whenever possible. **Depth-First Search (DFS)** explores edges adjacent to the most recently discovered vertex *v* that still has unexplored edges whose head is adjacent to it. Once all of *v*'s edges have been explored, the search "backtracks" to explore edges, leaving the vertex from which *v* was discovered. The process continues until all vertices that are reachable from the original source vertex have been discovered.

If any undiscovered vertices remain, then DFS selects one of them as a new source, and it repeats the search from that source. While it may seem odd that BFS limits itself to vertices reachable from a single source whereas DFS considers multiple sources, the reason behind it is related to the applications of these searches.

BFS is usually used to find shortest-path distances while DFS is often used as a subroutine in another algorithm, which we shall see when we explore the cycle detection problem.

Similar to BFS, when we discover a vertex v during the scan of the adjacency list of an already discovered vertex, we record its parent attribute. Since we mentioned that we explore different sources, the parent subgraph produced by DFS is, unlike the breadth-first tree, a forest (that is, a set of trees). In order to illustrate this, let's look at a run of DFS for the directed graph of Figure 6.1, starting at *node 2*, in the **Table 6.4**.

Table 6.4 A Run of DFS on the directed graph of Figure 6.1, Starting at Node 2

Step	Current Node	Discovered	Expanded	Undiscovered	Forest
0	2	{2}	{}	{0, 1, 3, 4, 5}	
1	4	{2, 4}	{}	{0, 1, 3, 5}	
2	3	{2, 4, 3}	{}	{0, 1, 5}	
3	1	{2, 4, 3, 1}	{}	{0, 5}	
4	3	{2, 4, 3, 1}	{1}	{0, 5}	

Step	Current Node	Discovered	Expanded	Undiscovered	Forest
5	4	{2, 4, 3, 1}	{1, 4}	{0, 5}	
6	2	{2, 4, 3, 1}	{1, 4, 3}	{0, 5}	
6	5	{2, 4, 3, 1, 5}	{1, 4, 3}	{0}	
7	2	{2, 4, 3, 1, 5}	{1, 4, 3, 5}	{0}	

Step	Current Node	Discovered	Expanded	Undiscovered	Forest
8	0	{2, 4, 3, 1, 5, 0}	{1, 4, 3, 5, 2}	{}	
9	-	{2, 4, 3, 1, 5, 0}	{1, 4, 3, 5, 2, 0}	{}	

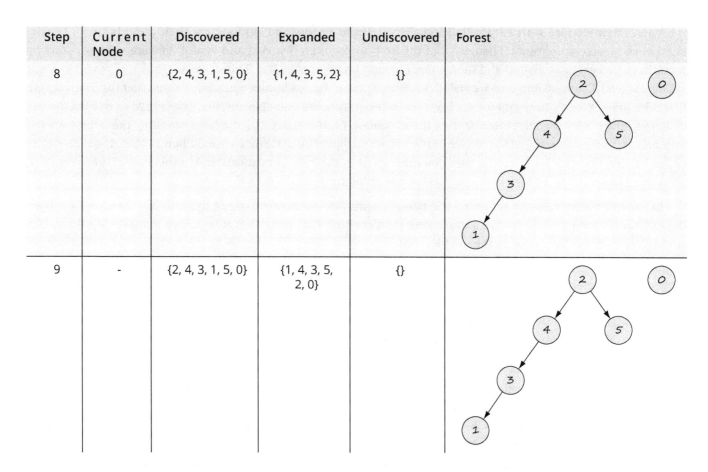

Note that the results of DFS may depend on the order in which the vertices are examined. In the previous case, we started with 2 and always went for the lowest-numbered vertex in the adjacency list of a vertex first. If we had started with *vertex 0*, we would have a different forest. In practice, we can usually use any DFS result with equivalent results.

We previously saw how to perform DFS on trees. DFS on graphs is similar, but we need to keep track of explored nodes so that we don't get stuck in cycles.

In order to implement DFS, we will assume that our graph is represented using adjacency lists. We will attach certain attributes to each vertex in the graph, which will allow us to guide our search and later construct the depth-first forest. **Snippet 6.5** illustrates the implementation of depth-first search.

Snippet 6.5   Implementation of depth-first search. Source class name: `dfs.Graph`.

```java
public void dfsVisit(int u, boolean[] visited, int[] parent) {
    visited[u] = true;
    for (int i = 0; i < adj[u].size(); i++) {
        int next = adj[u].get(i);
        if (!visited[next]) {
            parent[next] = u;
            dfsVisit(next, visited, parent);
        }
    }
}
```

The DFS procedure works by initializing all vertices as not visited, and setting their parents to -1 (meaning that they have no parent). Then, we find the first undiscovered vertex and visit it. In each visit, we start by recording the vertex as visited and then going through its adjacency list. There, we are looking for vertices not yet discovered. Once we find one, we visit it. Looking at the previous implementation, we see that the loops inside DFS take time $O(V)$, as they run for each vertex in the graph. We can also see that the `dfsVisit()` method is called exactly once for each vertex. During the execution of `dfsVisit()`, the loop scanning the adjacency list executes in time proportional to the size of the vertex's adjacency list. Since we said before that `dfsVisit()` is called exactly once for each vertex, the total time spent in the loop is proportional to the sum of the sizes of all adjacency lists, that is, $O(E)$. Therefore, the total running time of DFS is $O(V + E)$.

In the DFS method, we're returning the parent array, but the return type of this routine is usually adapted depending on the larger task that a more general algorithm that uses DFS is trying to achieve. We'll see DFS adapted to our specific needs in the next lesson.

Lesson 6.2.3 Cycle Detection

A useful application of DFS is determining whether or not a graph is acyclic (that is, it does not contain cycles). In order to do so, it's important to define four types of edges in terms of the depth-first forest produced by DFS. They are as follows:

- **Tree edges:** They are edges in the depth-first forest. An edge can only be a tree edge if it was the one explored when first discovering a vertex.
- **Back edges:** They are edges connecting a vertex to an ancestor in a depth-first tree. Self-loops (which may occur in directed graphs) are back edges.
- **Forward edges:** They are edges that do not belong to a depth-first tree but connect a vertex to one of its descendants in a depth-first tree. Forward edges are therefore edges that weren't used when performing the DFS, but connect vertices u and v in a depth-first tree provided that v is a descendant of u in the tree.
- **Cross edges:** They are all other edges. They can go between vertices in the same depth-first tree or they can go between vertices in different depth-first trees. They are therefore edges that weren't used when performing the depth-first search, but connect vertices that don't share an ancestor relationship in the same tree or vertices in different trees.

Having classified edges, it is possible to show that a directed graph is acyclic if and only if a DFS does not produce back edges. If a depth-first search produces a back *edge* (u, v), then vertex v is an ancestor of vertex u in the depth-first forest. Therefore, G contains a path from v to u, and (u, v) completes a cycle. This algorithm is generalizable for undirected graphs. In undirected graphs, if we find a back edge (u, v) and v is not the parent of u in the depth-first forest, then we are in the presence of a cycle.

> Test yourself by completing Lab Activity 6.2: Using BFS to Find the Shortest Path Out of a Maze.

In this lesson, we've introduced two different ways to traverse a graph – breadth-first search (BFS) and depth-first search (DFS). We've seen how to use BFS to find the single-source shortest path in unweighted graphs and how to use DFS to find cycles in a graph. In the next lesson, we will be looking at two different algorithms to find shortest paths in a graph.

LESSON 6.3 CALCULATING SHORTEST PATHS

The shortest path is a path between two vertices so that the sum of the weights of the edges that constitute the path is minimized. The shortest path problem has many applications in the real world, from finding directions on mapping applications to minimizing the moves to solve a puzzle.

In this lesson, we shall look at two different strategies for computing shortest paths: one that finds the shortest paths from a single source to every other vertex in the graph, and another that finds shortest paths between all pairs of vertices in a graph.

Lesson 6.3.1 Single Source Shortest Path: Dijkstra's Algorithm

When we explored BFS, we saw that it was able to solve the shortest path problem for unweighted graphs, or graphs whose edges have the same (positive) weight. What if we are dealing with weighted graphs? Can we do better? We shall see that Dijkstra's algorithm provides an improvement over the ideas presented in BFS and that it is an efficient algorithm for solving the single-source shortest path problem.

One restriction for working with Dijkstra's algorithm is that edges' weights have to be positive. This is usually not a big issue since most graphs represent entities modelled by edges with positive weights. Nonetheless, there are algorithms capable of solving the problem for negative weights. Since the use case for negative edges is less common, those algorithms are outside the scope of this course.

Dijkstra's algorithm, conceived by Edsger W. Dijkstra in 1956, maintains a set S of vertices whose final shortest-path weights from the source s have already been determined. The algorithm repeatedly selects the vertex u with the minimum shortest-path estimate, adds it to set S, and uses the outward edges from that vertex to update the estimates from vertices not yet in set S. In order to see this in action, let's consider the directed graph of **Figure 6.5**.

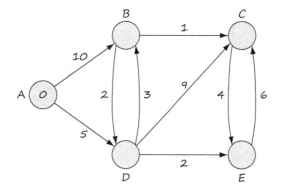

Figure 6.5   A Sample weighted directed graph

The graph is composed of five vertices (A, B, C, D, and E) and 9 edges. We're interested in finding the shortest paths, starting at vertex A. Note that A is already marked as 0, meaning that the current distance from A to A is zero. The other vertices don't have distances associated with them yet. It is common to use an estimate of infinity as the starting estimate for the distance of nodes not yet seen. **Table 6.5** shows a run of Dijkstra's algorithm for the graph of **Figure 6.5**, identifying the current vertex being selected and how it updates the estimates for vertices not yet seen.

Table 6.5   A Run of Dijkstra's algorithm for the weighted directed graph of Figure 6.5

Step	Explanation
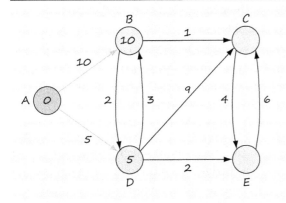 *(top diagram)*	Vertex A is the vertex with the lowest estimate weight, so it is selected as the next vertex whose edges are to be considered to improve our current estimates.
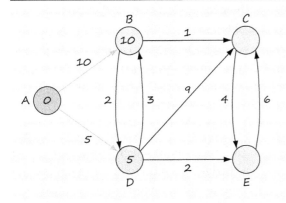	We use the outward edges from vertex A to update our estimates for vertices B and D. Afterwards, we add A to set S, avoiding a repeated visit to it. From the edges not yet visited, the one with the lowest estimate is now D, which shall be selected to visit next. Note that we also mark those edges that belong to our estimate shortest path in bold.
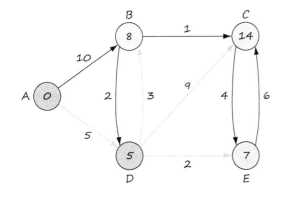	By exploring the outward edges from vertex D, we were able to improve our estimate for vertex B, so we update it accordingly and now consider a different edge for the shortest path. We were also able to discover vertices C and E, which become potential candidates to visit next. Since E is the one with the shorter estimate weight, we visit it next.
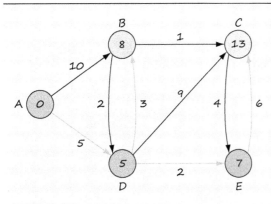	Using an outward edge from vertex E, we were able to improve our estimate for vertex C, and now look at vertex B as our next vertex to visit. Note that those vertices that belong to set S (shown in black in the figure) already have their shortest path computed. The value inside them is the weight of the shortest path from A to them, and you can follow the edges in bold to build the shortest path.

Step	Explanation
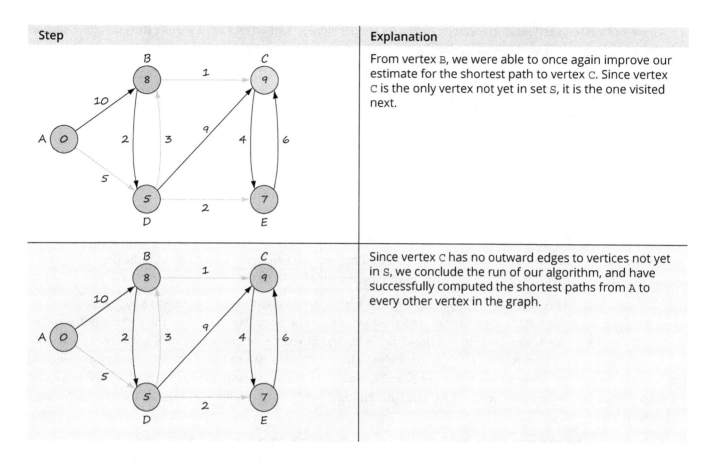	From vertex B, we were able to once again improve our estimate for the shortest path to vertex C. Since vertex C is the only vertex not yet in set S, it is the one visited next.
	Since vertex C has no outward edges to vertices not yet in S, we conclude the run of our algorithm, and have successfully computed the shortest paths from A to every other vertex in the graph.

Now that we've seen a run of Dijkstra's algorithm, let's try to put it in code and analyze its runtime performance. We will use an adjacency list representation for our graph, as it helps us when trying to explore the outward edges of a given vertex. The following code snippet shows a possible implementation of Dijkstra's algorithm as previously described:

Snippet 6.6   Implementation of Dijkstra's algorithm. Source class name: `Dijkstra`

```
while (!notVisited.isEmpty()) {
    Vertex v = getBestEstimate(notVisited);
    notVisited.remove(v);
    visited.add(v);
    for (Edge e : adj[v.u]) {
        if (!visited.contains(e.v)) {
            Vertex next = vertices[e.v];
            if (v.distance + e.weight < next.distance) {
                next.distance = v.distance + e.weight;
                parent[next.u] = v.u;
            }   }
    }   }
```

The *Dijkstra* method starts by initializing two sets:

• One for visited vertices
• One for unvisited vertices

The set of visited vertices corresponds to the set we previously named as *S*, and we use the one of not visited vertices to keep track of vertices to explore.

We then initialize each vertex with an estimated distance equal to `Integer. MAX_VALUE`, representing a value of "infinity" for our use case. We also use a *parent* array to keep track of parent vertices in the shortest path, so that we can later recreate the path from the source to each vertex.

The main loop runs for each vertex, while we still have vertices not yet visited. For each run, it selects the "best" vertex to explore. In this case, the "best" vertex is the one with the smallest distance of the vertices not visited so far (the `getBestEstimate()` function simply scans all vertices in the `notVisited()` set for the one satisfying the requirement).

Then, it adds the vertex to the set of visited vertices and updates the estimate distances for not visited vertices. When we run out of vertices to visit, we build our paths by recursively visiting the parent array.

Analyzing the runtime of the previous implementation, we can see that we have an initialization step that's proportional to the number of vertices in the graph, hence running in $O(V)$.

The main loop of the algorithm runs once for each vertex, so it is bounded by at least $O(V)$. Inside the main loop, we determine the next vertex to visit and then scan its adjacency list to update the estimate distances. Updating the distances takes time proportional to $O(1)$, and since we scan each vertex's adjacency list only once, we take time proportional to $O(E)$, updating estimate distances. We're left with the time spent selecting the next vertex to visit. Unfortunately, the `getBestEstimate()` method needs to scan through all the unvisited vertices, and is therefore bounded by $O(V)$. The total running time of our implementation of Dijkstra's algorithm is therefore $O(V^2 + E)$.

Even though some parts of our implementation seem difficult to optimize, it looks like we can do better when selecting the next vertex to visit. If we could have access to a data structure that was capable of storing our vertices sorted by lower estimated distance and provided efficient insert and remove operations, then we could reduce the $O(V)$ time spent inside the `getBestEstimate` method. In *Lesson 4, Algorithm Design Paradigms,* we briefly discussed a data structure used in *Huffman coding* named the priority queue, which is just what we need for this job. **Snippet 6.7** implements a more efficient version of Dijkstra's algorithm, using a priority queue.

Snippet 6.7   Implementation of Dijkstra's algorithm using a priority queue. Source class name: `DijkstraWithPQ`

```
PriorityQueue<Node> pq = new PriorityQueue<>();
pq.add(new Node(source, 0));
while (!pq.isEmpty()) {
    Node v = pq.remove();
    if (!vertices[v.u].visited) {
        vertices[v.u].visited = true;
        for (Edge e : adj[v.u]) {
            Vertex next = vertices[e.v];
            if (v.distance + e.weight < next.distance) {
                next.distance = v.distance + e.weight;
                parent[next.u] = v.u;
                pq.add(new Node(next.u, next.distance));
            }  }
    }  }
```

In this second implementation, we no longer keep sets for visited and not visited vertices. Instead, we rely on a priority queue that will be storing our distance estimates while we run the algorithm.

When we are exploring the outward edges from a given vertex, we therefore add a new entry to the priority queue in case we are able to improve our distance estimate.

Adding and removing an element from our priority queue takes $O(\log N)$ time, N being the number of elements in the queue. Do note that we can have the same vertex inserted more than once in the priority queue. That's why we check if we've visited it before expanding its edges.

Since we will visit the instance for that vertex with shorter estimate distance, it's safe to ignore the ones that come after it. However, that means that operations on our priority queue are not bounded by $O(\log V)$, but $O(\log E)$ instead (assuming that there's a connected graph). Therefore, the total runtime of this implementation is $O((V + E) \log E)$. It's still possible to improve this running time by using a priority queue implementation with better asymptotic bounds (such as a Fibonacci heap), but its implementation is out of the scope of this course.

One last thing to note about Dijkstra's algorithm is how it borrows ideas from BFS (the algorithm structure is very similar to Dijkstra's, but we end up using a priority queue instead of a normal queue) and that it is a very good example of a greedy algorithm: Dijkstra's algorithm makes the locally optimum choice (for example, it chooses the vertex with the minimum estimated distance) in order to arrive at a global optimum.

Lesson 6.3.2 All Pairs Shortest Paths: Floyd-Warshall Algorithm

Sometimes, it might be necessary to compute the shortest paths between all pairs of vertices. For example, we might be interested in building a table of distances. One way to do that is to perform a single source shortest path for every vertex of the graph. If you use Dijkstra's algorithm for that, we end up with a runtime of $O(V^* (V + E) \log E)$.

In this lesson, we shall explore an algorithm capable of solving the all pairs shortest paths problem in $O(V^3)$ time, with a remarkably simple and elegant implementation.

> **NOTE** The algorithm we are about to study, more commonly referred to as the Floyd-Warshall algorithm, was published in its current form by Robert Floyd in 1962. However, in its essence, it follows the same ideas published by Bernard Roy in 1959 and Stephen Warshall in 1962.

The algorithm uses the adjacency matrix representation and follows a dynamic programming approach. The basic idea behind it is that, when we're trying to compute the shortest-path distance between vertex i and vertex j, we try to use an intermediate vertex, k. We want to use an intermediate vertex so that doing the path from i to k and then from k to j shortens the currently computed shortest path between i and j. If we find such a vertex, then the best path we're able to compute so far between i and j must go through k. All that we need to do is, for each k, see if using it improves the shortest path between i and j, for all possible i and j.

In order to see that in practice, let's use the directed graph of Figure 6.5 that we used to illustrate Dijkstra's algorithm. The graph of Figure 6.5 has the adjacency matrix representation of **Table 6.6**.

Table 6.6 Adjacency matrix representation of the directed graph of Figure 6.5

	A	B	C	D	E
A	0	10	∞	5	∞
B	∞	0	1	2	∞
C	∞	∞	0	∞	4
D	∞	3	9	0	2
E	∞	∞	6	∞	0

The adjacency matrix representation serves as the starting point for the Floyd-Warshall algorithm, and we iterate through it until we're left with a matrix of the weights of the shortest paths between each pair of vertices. In order to do so, let's start with vertex A, considering it as an intermediate vertex for shortest paths. Unfortunately, vertex A doesn't have inward edges, meaning that it can't be used as an intermediate vertex for shortest paths. Using vertex B, we can improve the distance from A to C $(10 + 1) < \infty)$, and we can use it to go from A to D, but not improve the overall distance. We can also use it to improve the distance from D to C $(3 + 1 < 9)$. Therefore, after considering B as an intermediate vertex, we're left with the distance matrix of **Table 6.7**.

Table 6.7   Distance matrix after considering B as an intermediate vertex

	A	B	C	D	E
A	0	10	11	5	∞
B	∞	0	1	2	∞
C	∞	∞	0	∞	4
D	∞	3	4	0	2
E	∞	∞	6	∞	0

Now, we are going to look at vertex C. Using vertex C, we can improve the distance from A to E $(11 + 4 < \infty)$ and B to E $(1 + 4 < \infty)$ shown in **Table 6.8**.

Table 6.8   Distance matrix after considering C as an intermediate vertex

	A	B	C	D	E
A	0	10	11	5	15
B	∞	0	1	2	5
C	∞	∞	0	∞	4
D	∞	3	4	0	2
E	∞	∞	6	∞	0

Using vertex D, we can improve the distance from A to B $(5 + 3 < 10)$, A to C $(5 + 4 < 11)$, A to E $(5 + 2 < 15)$, and B to E $(2 + 2 < 5)$ shown in **Table 6.9**.

Table 6.9   Distance matrix after considering D as an intermediate vertex

	A	B	C	D	E
A	0	8	9	5	7
B	∞	0	1	2	4
C	∞	∞	0	∞	4
D	∞	3	4	0	2
E	∞	∞	6	∞	0

Using vertex E, we cannot improve any distance, so Table 6.9 already has the weights for the shortest paths between all pairs of vertices.

Implementing the Floyd-Warshall algorithm is very simple, as **Snippet 6.8** demonstrates.

Snippet 6.8   Implementation of Floyd Warshall's algorithm. Source class name: `FloydWarshall`

```java
public void run() {
    for (int k = 0; k < adj.length; k++) {
        for (int i = 0; i < adj.length; i++) {
            if (adj[i][k] >= Integer.MAX_VALUE)
                continue;
            for (int j = 0; j < adj.length; j++) {
                if (adj[k][j] >= Integer.MAX_VALUE)
                    continue;
                adj[i][j] = Math.min(adj[i][j], adj[i][k] + adj[k][j]);
            }
        }
    }
}
```

Looking at the implementation, the runtime of $O(V^3)$ becomes obvious. One alternative to the Floyd-Warshall algorithm is running Dijkstra's algorithm for each vertex in the graph (so that we end up with all pairwise shortest paths). Given that its complexity is closer to multiple applications of Dijkstra's algorithm for dense graphs, the Floyd-Warshall algorithm is frequently used in practice.

Test yourself by completing Lab Activity 6.3: Improving Floyd-Warshall's Algorithm to Reconstruct the Shortest Path.

In this lesson, we've introduced the shortest paths problem and visited two different algorithms to solve it: one for single source shortest paths (Dijkstra's algorithm), and another for all pairs shortest paths (Floyd-Warshall). We've shown how different implementations of Dijkstra's algorithm can affect its running time. For both algorithms, we've also shown how to reconstruct shortest paths using a parent array and a predecessor matrix, respectively.

LESSON 6.4 PRIME NUMBERS IN ALGORITHMS

A prime number is a natural number greater than one whose only divisors are one and the number itself.

Prime numbers play a very important role in the fundamental theorem of arithmetic: every natural number greater than one is either a prime or a product of primes. Nowadays, number-theoretic algorithms are widely used, mainly due to cryptographic schemes based on large prime numbers. Most of those cryptographic schemes are based on the fact that we can efficiently find large primes, but we cannot factor the product of those large primes efficiently.

Lesson 6.4.1 Sieve of Eratosthenes

The sieve of Eratosthenes is a simple and ancient algorithm to find all prime numbers up to a given limit. If we want to find all prime numbers up to N, we start by creating a list of consecutive integers from 2 to $N(2, 3, 4, 5 ... N)$, initially unmarked. Let's use p to denote the smallest unmarked number. Then, we select the smallest unmarked number p that is larger than the last p. In the first iteration, p will be two. Afterward, by increments of p, we mark elements in the list from $2p$ until Mp so that $Mp <= N$.

We repeat this strategy until it is impossible to mark more numbers in the list. At the end of the run, all the unmarked numbers are prime numbers. It is easy to see that all unmarked numbers will be the ones for which we couldn't find a divisor other than the number itself and 1, and are therefore prime numbers.

Lesson 6.4.2 Prime Factorization

Prime factorization is determining the prime factors of a given number. It is very difficult to build a general-purpose algorithm for this computationally hard problem. A general purpose algorithm that is commonly used to factorize primes was introduced in Module 1, Algorithms and Complexities. Its basic idea is to iterate through possible factors attempting to divide the number.

Start with 2; while the number is divisible by 2, keep dividing it, and add 2 to the list of factors. Afterwards, the number must be odd, so start a loop that checks for possible factors from 3 to the square root of the number.

Since we've already covered even numbers, you can do increments of 2 in this loop (there's no need to check 4, 6, 8, and so on once you've already checked 2). Once you find a suitable divisor, add the number to the list of factors and divide it until it is possible. At the end of this step, if we are left with a number greater than 2, then it is a prime number and therefore a prime factor of itself.

> Test yourself by completing Lab Activity 6.4: Implementing the Sieve of Eratosthenes.

LESSON 6.5 OTHER CONCEPTS IN GRAPHS

In this lesson, we covered ways of representing and traversing a graph and looked at shortest path algorithms. Graphs are also an optimal data structure for some problems we haven't mentioned yet. This lesson aims to introduce some of them.

Lesson 6.5.1 Minimum Spanning Trees

A minimum spanning tree of a graph is a subset of the set of edges E of a connected graph that connects all vertices together, without any cycles and with the minimum total edge weight. It is a tree because every two vertices in it are connected by exactly one path.

In order to understand the applicability of minimum spanning trees, consider the problem of a telecommunications company that is moving into a new neighborhood. The company wants to connect all the houses, but also wants to minimize the length of cable that it uses in order to cut costs. One way to solve the problem is by computing the minimum spanning tree of a graph whose vertices are the houses of the neighborhood, and the edges between houses are weighted according to the distance between them.

There are many algorithms to solve the minimum spanning tree problem. Two of the most famous are Prim's and Kruskal's.

Prim's algorithm is a greedy algorithm that repeatedly selects the edge of smaller weights that connect some edge not yet in the spanning tree with some edge already in the spanning tree. Its runtime depends on the implementation, but it's possible to achieve a runtime of $O(V \log E)$. It can be implemented similarly to Dijkstra's algorithm. We start with one vertex chosen arbitrarily to be part of the tree. All edges that connect to this "starting" vertex are added to a set of candidate edges that are sorted according to the edges' weights. While we still have vertices to add to the tree, we repeatedly select the edge with the smaller weight from the list of candidate edges that connects to a vertex not yet in the tree, and repeat the process for the new vertex.

Kruskal's algorithm is also a greedy algorithm that uses a disjoint-set data structure. A disjoint-set data structure, or union-find data structure, is a data structure that tracks elements that are partitioned into a number of non-overlapping subsets. It provides an efficient way to merge two sets and check whether two elements belong to the same set. The idea of Kruskal's algorithm is to reduce a forest (for example, a set of trees) to a single tree, using a disjoint-set data structure to keep track of trees. We start with one tree for each vertex, including only one vertex. While we have more than one tree, we select the edge of the smallest weight that connects two different trees (we don't want to produce a cycle), and join the two trees together. At the end, the resultant tree will be the one whose total edge weight is minimized. The running time of Kruskal's algorithm is also $O(V\log E)$.

Lesson 6.5.2 A* Search

The A* search algorithm is a very common algorithm when solving pathfinding problems. It also solves the shortest path problem, enhancing Dijkstra's algorithm with the introduction of a heuristic to guide the search. A heuristic is a practical estimate of a given cost, not guaranteed to be optimal or perfect, but sufficient for the immediate goals, or to guide a search. Its basic idea is that, when adding this heuristic to the estimated distance already computed for a node, one can guide the search toward the goal and avoid visiting certain vertices. For example, if we use the Euclidean distance (for example, the straight line distance between two points) from our location to the exit of a given maze, we can guide the search toward that and avoid visiting certain unnecessary positions.

Lesson 6.5.3 Maximum Flow

Some directed weighted graphs can be seen as flow networks. In a flow network, edge weights represent capacities and each edge receives a flow that can't exceed the edge's capacity. The maximum flow attempts to find a feasible flow through the network that is maximum, considering a single source (where the initial flow starts) and single sink (where the flow ends). The maximum flow problem allows one to solve related problems like pair wise assignment. There are various algorithms to solve the maximum flow problem. Three of the most famous ones are the Ford-Fulkerson algorithm, the Edmonds-Karp algorithm, and Dinic's algorithm.

The idea behind the Ford-Fulkerson algorithm is to repeatedly find augmenting paths in the flow network. An augmenting path is a path that still has an available capacity. While it is possible to find augmenting paths, one can add a flow through the path equal to its capacity and repeat the process. Ford-Fulkerson algorithm runs in $O(Ef)$, f being the maximum flow of the graph. The Edmonds-Karp algorithm improves on the Ford-Fulkerson algorithm by always selecting the augmenting path that is shortest. The runtime complexity of the Edmonds-Karp algorithm is $O(VE^2)$, independent of the maximum flow value. Dinic's algorithm runs in $O(V^2E)$ time, also building on shortest augmenting paths, but uses some concepts that make it more suitable for sparse graphs.

LESSON 6.6 UNDERSTANDING COMPLEXITY CLASSES OF PROBLEMS

Nearly all of the algorithms introduced so far run in polynomial time (for instance, on inputs of size n, their worst-case running time is $O(n^k)$ for constant k). However, there are problems that simply cannot be solved or for which a polynomial-time algorithm hasn't been found yet.

An example of a problem that cannot be solved is the halting problem. The halting problem is the problem of determining, from the description of a computer program and an input, whether the program will finish running or continue to run forever. Alan Turing proved that a general algorithm to solve the halting problem for all pairs of (program, input) cannot exist.

It is common to call problems solvable by polynomial-time algorithms (for instance, those whose worst-case running time is $O(n^k)$ for constant k) as "tractable," or "easy" and problems that require a super-polynomial-time algorithm (for instance, those whose running time is not bounded above by any polynomial) as "intractable," or "hard."

There is a class of problems, called **NP-Complete (NPC)** problems, and no one has yet found a polynomial-time algorithm to solve them. However, no one has yet been able to prove that no polynomial-time algorithm can exist for any of them.

There is another class of problems, called **NP** problems, whose solutions are verifiable in polynomial time. This means that, given a problem, and a possible solution to it, one can verify if the solution is correct in polynomial time.

All problems in P are also in NP. NPC consists of problems that belong to the NP class and to the NP-hard class. A problem is NP-hard if an algorithm for solving it can be translated into one for solving a NP problem.

One of the deepest open research problems in theoretical computer science is whether *P* is really different from *NP* (for instance, $P! = NP$).

Examples of NPC problems are as follows:

- Finding the longest path in the graph
- Finding a path in a graph that visits all vertices exactly once (known as a Hamiltonian path)

A common example of an NP-hard problem is finding the shortest path in a graph that visits all vertices exactly once and returns to the starting point. The problem consists of finding the Hamiltonian cycle of the smallest weight, and is often described as the traveling salesman problem as it models the problem of a salesman that needs to visit all cities and return to his hometown.

SUMMARY

In this module, we have introduced graphs, formalized what they are and shown two different ways to represent them in computer programs. Afterward, we took a look at ways of traversing graphs, using them as building blocks for building more complex algorithms on top. Then, we looked at two different algorithms for finding shortest paths in a graph.

We have briefly explored topics that logically follow the ones studied during this course. Even though they haven't been explored at a great level of detail, this lesson gives pointers for curious students to study on their own after these two days. The world of data structures and algorithms is vast and requires a type of mathematical reasoning for which some study and practice is required. However, one of the most rewarding feelings in the life of a software engineer is coming up with a clever algorithm to solve a hard problem.

Printed in the USA
CPSIA information can be obtained
at www.ICGtesting.com
BVHW022258040823
668258BV00008B/84